SHAKESPEAREAN GLEANINGS

AMS PRESS

NEW YORK

Enter Tamora pleadinge for her Sonnes
going to execution

HENRY PEACHAM'S ILLUSTRATION TO *TITUS ANDRONICUS*

SHAKESPEAREAN GLEANINGS

By
E. K. CHAMBERS

OXFORD UNIVERSITY PRESS
1944

Library of Congress Cataloging in Publication Data

Chambers, Sir Edmund Kerchever, 1866—1954.
 Shakespearean gleanings.

 1. Shakespeare, William, 1564—1616. I. Title.
PR2899.C4 1974   822.3'3   74-153312
ISBN 0-404-01444-5

This reprint has been authorized by the
Clarendon Press Oxford.

Reprinted with permission from a volume
in the Ohio State University Libraries.

Reprinted from the edition of 1944, Oxford
First AMS edition published in 1974
Manufactured in the United States of America

AMS PRESS, INC.
NEW YORK, N.Y. 10003

PREFATORY NOTE

HERE is another collection of studies, old and new. 'The Disintegration of Shakespeare' was a lecture before the British Academy, and was reprinted in *Aspects of Shakespeare* (Clarendon Press, 1933). 'The Unrest in Shakespearean Studies' was contributed to *The Nineteenth Century and After*. 'William Shakespeare: an Epilogue' was in its original form a lecture to students of the English School at Oxford. It became an article in the *Review of English Studies*, and has since undergone a slight revision. 'The Integrity of *The Tempest*' also made its appearance in that *Review*. 'The Occasion of *A Midsummer-Night's Dream*' was written for Dr. Gollancz's *A Book of Homage to Shakespeare*, 'The Stage of the Globe' for A. H. Bullen's *Stratford Town Shakespeare*, and 'The First Illustration to Shakespeare' for *The Library* (Bibliographical Society). 'Shakespeare at Corpus', a skit of my Oxford days, was printed in *The Pelican Record*. Gratitude for their hospitality is due to the editors and publishers of all these. The essays on 'William Shakeshafte', 'The Date of Hamlet', 'The Order of the Sonnets', 'The Youth of the Sonnets', and 'The Mortal Moon Sonnet' are recent work, and have not been printed before. Once again, in war-time, a salute here to the constant sympathy and patience of my wife must take the place of a dedicatory page.

E. K. C.

October 1943.

CONTENTS

THE DISINTEGRATION OF SHAKESPEARE

The rock of Shakespeare's reputation stands four-square to the winds of Time. But the waves of criticism beat perpetually about its base, and at intervals we must stand back and re-affirm our vision of the structural outlines. It is perhaps in itself a tribute to the wide appeal of the poet that so much of what is written about him is ill-informed and ill-balanced. Small minds are caught by, and fail to comprehend, that greatness and that variability. Hence the scouring of the *Dictionary of National Biography* for an alternative author, preferably aristocratic, of the plays. With these paradoxes I do not propose to concern myself. Doubtless they should be refuted, that the people be not deceived, but the task must be left to some one with a better temper for the patient anatomizing of human follies. This is but the spindrift on the face of the rock.

I propose to consider certain critical tendencies which, in their extreme manifestations, offer results hardly less perturbing than those with which the Baconians and their kin would make our flesh creep. This is the argument. Here are thirty-six plays handed down as Shakespeare's. You can put them in approximate chronological order, and arrive at a conception of the author's trend of development, both in mental outlook and in habits of diction and versification. But a closer analysis often reveals the co-existence in one and the same play of features belonging to different stages of the development, and sometimes of features which it is difficult to place in the line of development at all. Moreover, an examination of the texts shows such eccentricities and dislocations as to raise a doubt whether they can have come to us just as Shakespeare left them. Tracing these clues, our critics arrive at three results, on which varying degrees of stress are laid. Firstly, the extant texts, many of them not printed until several years after Shakespeare's death, have often been altered or abbreviated by other hands. Secondly, Shakespeare revised his plays, and the extant texts sometimes contain fragments of different recensions, in juxtaposition or overlay. Thirdly, the process of revision by Shakespeare was not confined to his own work; he also rehandled the work of other men, and left some or much of it standing in the texts. And if you ask how far this process of revision went, and whether it seriously qualifies the accepted Shakespearean authorship of the plays, you do not get reassuring answers. One man will tell you frankly that in many plays which you thought characteristically Shakespearean—*Richard II, Henry V, Julius Caesar,* for example—Shakespeare's part was quite subordinate. Another will fence with the issue, and explain that the conception of individual authorship is not altogether applicable to Elizabethan plays. The playing companies kept standing texts in their repertories, and one man after another brought them up to date, often over a long period of years, as theatrical needs required or literary fashions changed, so that a drama must really be thought of as an impersonal or communal affair, like a folk-lyric.

Well, you cannot brush away these speculations quite so easily as you can those of the Baconians. Keen wits are at work; well-equipped and painstaking minds have stated their theories —their heresies, if you will—and they demand scrutiny. We must follow the *Logos* where it leads. Obviously, one cannot take the matter far in an isolated lecture. Each of the impugned plays requires its individual examination. This must be based upon a patient analysis of the texts available. It must take account of what can be gleaned of the literary habits of the time; of the possibilities of sophistication latent in the activities of stage book-keepers and adapters, of copyists, of censors, of compositors and correctors of the press. The disintegrating critics give us no less; we owe them no less. I can only hope to make some general survey of the ground, and to chart some of the avenues of approach.

The traditional canon of the plays has a five-fold basis. Thirty-six plays were ascribed to Shakespeare in the First Folio. Thirteen of these had already been printed as his in Quarto. Eleven had been ascribed to him by Francis Meres in 1598. Five are ascribed to him by other contemporaries.[1] This is external evidence. There is also such internal evidence as the plays themselves bear to the presence of a single 'shaping spirit of imagination'. It is, of course, primarily this internal evidence which the disintegrators, at this and that point, dispute. The external evidence they have merely to explain away. You can always explain away an historical record, with a sufficient licence of conjecture as to the *mala fides* of its origin. The

---

[1] *Romeo and Juliet* and *Richard II* or *III*, by John Weever; *Hamlet,* by Gabriel Harvey; *Julius Caesar* and *Winter's Tale,* by Ben Jonson.

earliest whisper against the authenticity of any play in the canon comes, I think, from Edward Ravenscroft. Ravenscroft adapted *Titus Andronicus* after the Restoration, and, when he printed it in 1687, said that he had been told by 'some anciently conversant with the stage' that the model was not originally Shakespeare's, 'but brought by a private author to be acted, and he only gave some master touches to one or two of the principal parts or characters'.   We do not know who were Ravenscroft's informants. At least one old actor, William Beeston, whose father had been a 'fellow' of Shakespeare, and who may himself have known Shakespeare in his boyhood, survived to 1682. A true report is not, therefore, inconceivable. Eighteenth-century scepticism was not slow to seize upon this notion of revisional work by Shakespeare, and to give it a further extension.   You find the substantial Shakespearean authorship of *Comedy of Errors, Love's Labour's Lost,* and oddly enough *Winter's Tale,* doubted by Pope (1725), of *Henry V* by Theobald (1734), of *Two Gentlemen of Verona* by Hanmer (1743), of *Richard II* by Johnson (1765), of *Taming of the Shrew* by Farmer (1767).   It would be idle to raise the dust of the resultant controversies, in which the conservative side was taken by Edward Capell.   The assailants were confident and impressionist.   Ritson tells us that in *Two Gentlemen, Love's Labour's Lost,* and *Richard II,* 'Shakespeare's new work is as apparent as the brightest touches of Titian would be on the poorest performance of the veriest canvas spoiler that ever handled a brush'.   The mutterings were largely silenced by the authority of Malone, who accepted Ravenscroft's account of *Titus Andronicus,* worked out the relation of *2* and *3 Henry VI* to the *Contention* plays, took Shakespeare for their reviser, supposed *Henry VIII* to have undergone revision by a later hand, and beyond these only doubted *1 Henry VI,* the admission of which to the Folio he explained by Shakespeare's contribution of the Talbot scenes.   Pope and the rest had been misled by inadequate attention to the chronology of the plays, which Malone was himself the first to study in detail, and by a consequent failure to distinguish between the criteria applicable to Shakespeare's juvenile and to his mature work.   Malone's conclusions determined critical orthodoxy for the best part of a century.   There were individual dissentients, notably Coleridge, who questioned much of *Richard III* and the 'low soliloquy' of the Porter in *Macbeth,* and declared in his table-talk, 'I think

I could point out to half a line what is really Shakespeare's in *Love's Labour's Lost* and some other of the not entirely genuine plays'. Coleridge being Coleridge, it is needless to say that he never performed this task. Charles Knight (*c.* 1843) suggested that Shakespeare was only a reviser of *Timon of Athens*; James Spedding and Alfred Tennyson (*c.* 1850) fixed the second hand in *Henry VIII* as that of Fletcher; and William George Clark and William Aldis Wright (1874) elaborated Coleridge's heresy about *Macbeth* by ascribing substantial interpolations in that play to Middleton.

Modern criticism of the canon, however, mainly owes its origin to F. G. Fleay, whose views, after fluttering the dove-cotes of the New Shakspere Society, were collected in his *Shakespeare Manual* (1876), thereafter underwent Protean transformations, and took final shape in his *Life and Work of Shakespeare* (1886). Fleay had read widely in dramatic litera-ture, and had made a close study of the early texts, the diction, and particularly the versification, of Shakespeare. He came to distrust the received chronology, because it assigned single dates to plays which seemed to him to bear stylistic marks of more than one period. And he arrived at a theory of constant rehandling and of the co-existence in the texts of strata belong-ing to different dates. This he applied, at one time or another, and with frequent variations in the dates assigned, to thirteen of the thirty-six plays: *Comedy of Errors, Two Gentlemen, Love's Labour's Lost, Romeo and Juliet, Midsummer-Night's Dream, Richard II, Much Ado, Hamlet, Merry Wives, Twelfth Night, All's Well, Troilus and Cressida, Cymbeline.* As to the occasions of such revision he speaks with an uncertain voice. One group of plays may have been re-written, either for stage revival or for publication. Of another he suggests that fragments left un-finished at an early date were completed a decade later. But this notion is abandoned in favour of a supposed desire to replace work of an early coadjutor by Shakespeare's own. It is an easy step from Shakespeare as a reviser of Shakespeare to Shakespeare as a reviser of predecessors. Fleay distributed and redistributed *Henry VI, Richard III*, and *Titus Andronicus* among Shakespeare, Marlowe, Greene, Peele, Lodge, and Kyd; found much of Lodge and a little of Drayton in *Taming of the Shrew*, traces of Peele in *Romeo and Juliet*, traces of Kyd in *Hamlet*, debris of Dekker and Chettle in *Troilus and Cressida*. He pressed the doctrine of Middleton in *Macbeth*, but became

doubtful about it; thought the second hand in *Timon* Tour-
neur's, and dropped him lightly for Wilkins; supposed the
mask in *The Tempest* an interpolation by Beaumont. Perhaps
his most revolutionary hypothesis was upon *Julius Caesar*,
which he held to have been abridged and altered by Ben Jonson, as an appropriate return for an equally conjectural contribution by Shakespeare to a lost version of *Sejanus*. We approach
the point where scholarship merges itself in romance. I desire
to speak with respect and even kindness of Fleay, from whom,
in common in many others, I derived an early stimulus to these
studies. He was a man of fertile and ingenious mind. He laid
his finger upon many of the bibliographical and stylistic features
of the plays which loom large in current speculations. But he
had a demon of inaccuracy, which was unfortunate, as he relied
largely upon statistics. And he betrayed an imperfect sense of
responsibility, both in advancing destructive notions without
an adequate support of argument, and in withholding the explanations and justifications required by his own numerous and
sometimes disconcerting changes of opinion. His self-confi-
dence has hypnotized his successors, and many of his impro-
visations recur in the works of serious students, not to speak
of those school-books, compiled at starvation wages for com-
petitive publishers, which do so much in our day for the
dissemination of critical and historical error.

The mantle of Mr. Fleay has descended upon Mr. J. M.
Robertson, who disposes its flying skirts into the decent folds
of a logical system. His method of approach to his problems
is uniform. It has three stages, upon each of which I shall have
a cautionary note later. He begins with impressionist judgements. Certain passages do not answer to his conception of
Shakespeare. Here is braggadocio, there an archaic stiffness,
or flatness, or hackwork, or clumsy stage-craft, or pointless
humour, or turgidity of thought, or falsity of moral sentiment.
Or a whole play repels him. One reads like 'a mosaic of dis-
parate parts'; in another he gets 'a strange feeling' about the
general style. Then he proceeds to confirm his impressions by
applying what he calls the 'inexorable' tests of treatment,
style, and metrics; in particular, tests based upon the chronological phases of Shakespeare's blank verse. Finally, he settles
down to look for 'clues' to the possible presence of alien hands;
clues furnished by the use of words rare in Shakespeare's
vocabulary, but traceable in the writings of other men; clues

derived from characteristic tricks of phrase or tendencies in the handling of typical situations. It is all logical enough, given certain major premises, largely disputable. First you decide that Shakespeare cannot be present; then you look for the intruder. Mr. Robertson has now covered most of his ground, and tells us that, although he still has to dispose of *Cymbeline* and *The Tempest*, we are at a point where the 'idolater'—that is to say the man who believes in Shakespeare's authorship of the plays, more or less as they stand—'has probably heard what he would term "the worst"'. The worst, however, amounts to an alien invasion. In the front of a rather dim background of collaborations and revisions stand the two heroic figures, Marlowe and Chapman. I will disregard the ancient battle-fields of *Henry VI* and *Titus Andronicus*, for the campaign has now become more serious. If I understand Mr. Robertson aright, Marlowe, more than any other man, is predominantly the author of *Richard III*, *Richard II*, *Henry V*, *Julius Caesar*, and paradoxically enough *Comedy of Errors*, even in the forms in which they have reached us. Peele and Greene play minor parts, but the *Two Gentlemen* is substantially Greene's, and work of his remains embedded in *Taming of the Shrew* and *All's Well*. I gather that Peele is to be similarly revealed in *Cymbeline*. And both men, together with Kyd, Jonson, and the shades of many of Philip Henslowe's hungry troop of hack writers, Chettle, Dekker, Drayton, Heywood, and Munday, are evoked as possible contributors to a series of drafts and recasts, which the Marlovian work has undergone. Ultimately, of course, the Marlovian plays passed into the hands of Shakespeare, and they show traces of revision by him, which however was often limited to a little retouching or the insertion of particular speeches or scenes, 'substantially preserved' the original *Richard II*, and even in *Henry V* did not amount to 'vital rehandling'. Chapman, too, was among the intermediate manipulators of the earlier plays. But when Marlowe passes out of the chronicle, Chapman becomes a protagonist. His unquiet spirit flies like a lambent but smoky flame over all the later part of the canon. He may have inserted the mask into *The Tempest* after Shakespeare left it. But in the main his work underlies, rather than overlies, Shakespeare's, in the form of drafts or contributions to drafts of plays, sometimes themselves mere recasts, which Shakespeare afterwards rewrote as *Hamlet*, *Merry Wives*, *All's Well*, *Measure for Measure*, *Troilus and*

Cressida, Timon, and *Pericles.* To Chapman I will return. The complicated nature of Mr. Robertson's reconstructions and their relation to Fleay's may be illustrated by the case of *Julius Caesar.* Marlowe is conjectured to have written a sequence of three plays: a *Caesar and Pompey,* a *Caesar's Tragedy,* a *Caesar's Revenge.* These passed to the Admiral's men at the Rose, who revived *Caesar and Pompey* and *Caesar's Tragedy,* after some revision of the latter by Chapman and Drayton, as their two-part *Caesar and Pompey* of 1594–5. The first part was now laid aside and re-written later by Chapman as his *Caesar and Pompey,* printed in 1631. Marlowe's original third play, *Caesar's Revenge,* was perhaps recast by Dekker, Drayton, Middleton, Munday, and Webster, in the *Caesar's Fall* or *The Two Shapes,* which they wrote for the Admiral's in 1602. However this may be, the *Tragedy* and the *Revenge,* now containing the work of from three to seven hands, were transferred by the Admiral's to the Chamberlain's company, and were revised for the latter, still in a two-play form, by Shakespeare. Finally, perhaps about 1607, the two plays were compressed into the one now extant by Ben Jonson, who added some touches of his own in a characteristic anti-Caesarian vein. More of the present substance is allowed to Shakespeare than in some of the Marlovian plays retrieved from the canon by Mr. Robertson; but the primitive Marlowe still shows through the overlay, notably in the speeches of Antony over the body of Caesar. It is entertaining to find that another recent critic, Mr. William Wells, also traces the origin of *Julius Caesar* to Marlowe. But he ascribes the revision, not to Chapman or to Jonson, but to Francis Beaumont, and only allows Shakespeare the first fifty-seven lines of the play, lines which Mr. Robertson thinks un-Shakespearean. Evidently the disintegration of Shakespeare is an open career for talent.

Looking back over the results of Mr. Robertson's devastating offensive, I am tempted to quote my friend A. H. Bullen's comment upon a more modest raid. 'If this goes on,' he said, 'Shakespeare will soon, like his own Lord Timon,

> be left a naked gull,
> Which flashes now a phoenix.'

Mr. Robertson will certainly reply that, even if witty, this is not fair. He is no despoiler of Shakespeare's authentic plumage. His eliminations touch nothing 'save inferior or second-rate work'; have not 'impugned one of the great plays as a whole,

or a really great speech in any'. On the contrary, it is the
sticklers for the canon who detract from Shakespeare's greatness. Battling for quantity, they sacrifice quality. 'The *vin
ordinaire* of the Elizabethan drama is for them indistinguishable
from the vintage of the Master.' In particular, if they will not
recognize Marlowe in *Richard II* or Greene in the *Two Gentlemen*, they are driven back on the alternative theory of a Shakespeare in bondage to a humiliating trick of mimicry, a 'parrot'
Shakespeare, a 'sedulous ape'. This brings me to the first of
my cautionary notes upon the successive steps in Mr. Robertson's critical progress. They are, you remember, three; the
disquieting impressions, the 'inexorable' tests, the 'clues' to
other men. I am sure that Mr. Robertson desires to exalt and
not to depreciate Shakespeare. And that is precisely where the
mischief lies. Our heresiarch, in fact, is himself an idolater.
We have all of us, in the long run, got to form our conception
of the 'authentic' Shakespeare by means of an abstraction from
the whole of the canon; there is no other material. Mr. Robertson abstracts through a series of rejections. He is repelled by
childish work, by imitative work, by repetitive work, by conventional work, by unclarified work, by clumsy construction,
by baldness or bombast. He idealizes. He looks for a Shakespeare always at the top of his achievement. This seems to me
quite an arbitrary process. I cannot so read the record. Magic
of phrase, lyrical impulse, pervasive humour, intuition of
character, the clash of drama, a questing philosophy, a firm
hold on the ultimate values of life: you are never far from one
or other of these at any turn in Shakespeare. But these are not
the whole warp and woof of the plays. We cannot be blind to
the moments of artistic oblivion or carelessness, where the
brain flags or the insight fails; to the trivial scenes where
quibble speaks to the boxes or horse-play to the pit; to the
exasperating scenes where psychological realism makes ugly
nonsense of a romantic convention; to the perfunctory scenes
which amount to no more than commonplace Elizabethan
dramatic carpentry. We cannot leave these out of the account;
if we do, we may get an ideal, but we lose Shakespeare. Of
course I can construct apologies. There are inconsistencies of
narrative and time-sequence. A practical playwright knows
very well that these attract little attention on the stage, although
they reveal themselves to the student poring over a printed text
in his study. There are jests and wit-combats which do not

seem to have the ghost of a laugh left in them. What is there so fleeting, so difficult to transmit from one age to another, as that phosphoric iridescence upon the surface of social life which we call wit? But I am not looking for apologies. I come to accept Shakespeare, not to praise him. Obviously there are things in the plays which any other Elizabethan could just as well, or just as badly, have written. They do not perturb me, as they perturb Mr. Robertson, to the point of searching for clues to another man. Perhaps Mr. Robertson will reply that I have not fully met his case; that it is not so much the passages of unmannered carpenter's work which give him pause, as passages which have a manner, but a manner which he cannot feel to be Shakespeare's, and does feel, when he analyses it, to be that of a Marlowe or of a Chapman. Here we are on more difficult ground. But it is part of the character of Shakespeare, as I read it in the canon, to be an experimentalist in style. I cannot regard the many phases through which his writing went in the short span of some twenty years as wholly due to a growth in which there was nothing deliberate. I discern abrupt beginnings and abrupt discontinuances. And he was receptive, as well as creative. I can suppose him experimenting in the manner of Marlowe, or even of poor Greene. And I can suppose him, much later, playing with stylistic elements, which had struck him in the work of Chapman, and ultimately dismissing them as, on the whole, unprofitable.

We come now to the 'inexorable' tests. These are largely metrical, based upon the familiar tables, compiled by Fleay and others, which put in statistical form the relative frequencies in each play of certain features of Shakespeare's versification, and notably the percentages of rhymes, double endings, and overflowing lines. I do not undervalue these features as elements in determining the chronology of the plays. No doubt there was a period—not, I think, his earliest period—in which Shakespeare made free use of rhyme; and thereafter even occasional rhymes dwindle. Even more important is an increasing tendency to escape from the tyranny of the 'drumming decasyllabon', and to emphasize the verse paragraph rather than the individual line, by the help of such devices as the double ending and a varied and subtle distribution of pauses. The tables need to be used with great discretion. Fleay's methods, in particular, were never 'inexorable'. His earliest tables were grossly inaccurate. He published a revised set, obscurely, in the book of another man.[1] I have spent much time, which might, perhaps, have been better employed, in checking some of these. They are still inaccurate, but less so. It is disquieting to find that little handbooks of facts about Shakespeare, compiled by distinguished scholars, still reproduce the unrevised tables as authoritative. Other tables, due to Goswin König, give only ratios and not the counts upon which they are based. This does not inspire confidence. If statistical precision were material, the calculations would probably have to be done afresh. I do not think that it is material. The tests cannot give an exact chronology; in fact, different tests do not give the same chronology. They can only indicate a trend of development, and the trend may be diverted in any play by accidents of subject-matter, such as refractory personal names which have to be coerced into the metre; by the appropriateness of particular rhythms to scenes of particular temper; above all, by Shakespeare's experimentalism, which certainly extends to rhythm. It does not therefore trouble me to find a rather high percentage of double endings in such early plays as *Comedy of Errors* and *Two Gentlemen of Verona*, and then to find the curve dropping through *Midsummer-Night's Dream*, *King John*, and *1 Henry IV*, and then rising again with *2 Henry IV* and other plays. But it does trouble Mr. Robertson, and, as he is debarred from putting *Comedy of Errors* and *Two Gentlemen* later in the chronological order, because that would throw out the overflow curve, he falls back upon a theory that they are mainly the work of other writers with metrical habits different from Shakespeare's. This longing for a smoothly progressive curve is only one aspect of a general tendency to seek an unimpeded development in Shakespeare's art. There is a philosophical predisposition behind. Mr. Robertson dislikes the idea of what he calls a 'cerebral cataclysm'. To suppose that Shakespeare passed suddenly from the merely average and imitative merit of *Two Gentlemen* to the 'supreme poetic competence' of *Midsummer-Night's Dream* is contrary to a doctrine which sees in 'artistic growth as in other organic phenomena a process of evolution'. I do not know whether the latest theories of organic evolution have solved that old *crux* of the emergence of variations. But in any case biological analogies do not help us very directly in analysing the development of the creative impulse in human consciousness. And when Mr. Robertson expresses

---

[1] C. M. Ingleby, *Shakespeare, the Man and the Book*, Part II (1881).

himself as taken aback by the notion of 'a literary miracle of genius elicited by some sudden supernatural troubling of the waters', I can only reply that he has given an admirable description of the way in which genius does in fact often appear to effloresce.

I have not quite done with the percentages. Obviously they have no value, unless they are worked upon a sufficient number of lines to allow a fair average to establish itself. This is common to all statistics. The ratio of blue eyes to black ones throughout England has a statistical meaning; the ratio in your house or mine may have a meaning, but it is not statistical. Possibly the two or three thousand lines of a play leave room for the averaging of double endings. But to work the percentage of double endings in a single speech or scene leads to nothing. Or rather, it should lead to nothing. It does sometimes lead Mr. Robertson to infer that scenes in a play which give very different percentages cannot have been written by the same hand, or at least by the same hand at the same date. Surely this is an illegitimate inference. If a play has twenty-five per cent. of double endings, they are not spread evenly at the rate of one double ending in every four lines.[1] They come in nuggets here; there are considerable spaces without them. Largely this is mere accident; they just fall so. But clearly that adaptation of rhythm to subject-matter, which may qualify the general trend of metric development in a whole play, is even more potent in single passages. Here are two examples. The first scene of *King John* is largely a discussion of the paternity of the Bastard Faulconbridge. And the rhetoric requires the emphatic use of the words 'father', 'mother', 'brother', at the ends of lines. These words account for about half the double endings in the scene, and the percentage, which for the play as a whole is 6, goes up in this scene to 16. Take again *Coriolanus*, a play which Mr. Robertson has not yet assailed, or expressed an intention of assailing. The double ending percentage is 28. But in v. 3 is a passage of twenty-four lines without one double ending and another of thirty-five lines with only three. One contains the stately interchange of courtesies between Coriolanus and his wife and mother on their entry to Corioli; the other the more solemn part of Volumnia's appeal to her son.

---

[1] I am told that the term 'double endings' puzzled some of my hearers. They are also called 'feminine endings', and are those in which the stressed second syllable of the last foot of a line is followed by an additional unstressed syllable.

Are these, therefore, un-Shakespearean or debris of early Shakespearean work?

My third cautionary note is on the final stage of Mr. Robertson's process, the quest for alien hands, with the clues of vocabulary and phraseology. Here I will be brief, for the land is unmapped and the footing treacherous. Are we really able to ascribe a distinctive diction to each of Shakespeare's predecessors? Do they not largely, together with the young Shakespeare himself, use a common poetic diction, much of it ultimately traceable to Spenser and to Sidney? We could tell better, if we knew more clearly what each of them wrote and did not write. The problem seems to me one which calls for exploration upon a general and disinterested method, rather than along the casual lines of advance opened up by the pursuit of an author for this or that suspected or anonymous play. The relation of Shakespeare's maturer diction to Chapman's is a problem of a somewhat different kind. There is not much point in a controversy as to which was the greater neologist. They both innovate freely, and apparently in much the same manner; and, as far as I know, Shakespeare at least was not likely to have had any scruple about using neologisms not of his own mintage. If he borrowed his plots, why should he not borrow his words? Nobody would suppose that he could not mint them fast enough, if he wanted to. It certainly does not move me to be told that Chapman must have worked over a scene, because it contains words not found elsewhere in Shakespeare, but found half a dozen times in Chapman. The oftener Chapman used a word, the more likely it was to stick in Shakespeare's memory. But Chapman is the recurrent *deus ex machina* of Mr. Robertson's speculations upon half a dozen plays of the canon. Writing about *Hamlet*, he formulates a theory of

A frequent employment of Chapman by Shakespeare's company either as a draftsman or as an adapter of plays, and as a 'repairer' or patcher of some; and the corollary that Shakespeare, often revising Chapman's work, which he must frequently have found trying, might very well let pass, as appealing to sections of the audience, *genre* and other work which he for his own part would never have thought of penning.

It all seems to have begun with *Timon*, and here a more intimate relation between the poets is revealed. *Timon* is a play 'imperfectly drafted' by Chapman and 'imperfectly revised' by Shakespeare. Mr. Robertson, like some others, thinks that Chapman was the 'rival poet' of the *Sonnets* and the Holophernes of *Love's Labour's Lost*. But this was merely a 'humorous quarrel with his testy rival', and after all the two men 'had a common patron', and 'there is no difficulty in conceiving that, with or without the patron's intervention, Shakespeare's company may have bought a play of Chapman's for Shakespeare to adapt'. We are bidden to remember that Chapman was poor and that Shakespeare must have seen that he was 'worth helping'. The greater poet had 'no artistic jealousy', and knew that 'the quality of mercy is not strained', and 'even if Chapman had ruffled him somewhat by his pedantic asperities, he of all men best knew the human struggle behind the "paste-board portico", the weakness under the shining armour of literary bravado'. Mr. Robertson is an austere rationalist, but I think that this little fantasy would have evoked comment even in the pages of Shakespeare's more sentimental biographers. However this may be, I find it difficult to fit this employment of Chapman by Shakespeare's company into the probabilities of literary history. We know a good deal about Chapman, at any rate from about 1596, when he begins to appear in Henslowe's diary. He wrote, or began to write, seven plays for the Admiral's men during the next three years, of which two were published, and one was a considerable financial success. And he is conspicuous in Henslowe's motley crew as the one who held most aloof from anything in the way of collaboration. The only exception is a play which he undertook, but quite possibly never finished, on a plot by Ben Jonson. About 1599 he drops out of Henslowe's record, and the next decade is covered by a long series of nine plays, all of which were published, for the boy companies. One of these was written in collaboration with Jonson and Marston. Thereafter, so far as we know, Chapman abandoned stage-writing, and devoted himself to his translation of Homer and to other non-dramatic work. In 1613, however, he did a mask for the Princess Elizabeth's wedding. He lived to 1634, and it is conceivable that in Caroline days he touched up some of his early plays, or lent a hand to the younger playwright, Shirley. The only trace of any external evidence for a connexion of Chapman with the Chamberlain's or King's men is the ascription to him by the publisher Moseley, in 1654, of *Alphonsus Emperor of Germany*. Hardly any one now believes that he wrote *Alphonsus*, which was produced at the Blackfriars in 1636, two years after his death, and twenty after Shakespeare's.

The Stationers' Register names the author as John Poole. All this is, of course, no proof that Chapman did not write for Shakespeare's company, concurrently with the Admiral's or the boys. A dramatist, who was not himself an actor, was not tied to a single paymaster. But Chapman was evidently a successful writer from 1596 onwards. He is one of the seven lauded by Webster in 1612. And it does not seem to me likely, on *a priori* grounds, that he would have needed Shakespeare's patronage for an introduction to the company; that no work done by him for them would have reached publication; that his temper would have submitted to constant revision by Shakespeare; or that, if his work proved unsatisfactory, the company would have continued the experiment over half a dozen plays.

I have slipped from the internal to the external evidence on the canon. Mr. Robertson is rather cavalier with the external evidence. Of the Folio editors he says:

> We may pardon the players for obstinately specifying as Shakespeare's works—in order to maintain their hold on the copyrights about which they are so obviously and so naturally anxious—a collection of plays as to which they knew and we know that much of the writing is not Shakespeare's at all.

I am not concerned to argue for the literal inspiration of the Folio. It is quite conceivable that in some cases a substantial Shakespearean contribution, short of full authorship, may have been held to justify the inclusion of a play. But it was certainly not an undiscriminating collection, since it left out, for one reason or another, no less than nine plays which had already been printed under Shakespeare's name or initials. And what has copyright to do with the matter? I do not know what copyright Mr. Robertson thinks that the players claimed in published plays; but, so far as our knowledge goes, no kind of printing copyright existed, which could be strengthened by ascribing a play to a particular author. As for Francis Meres, he, we are told, 'simply stated the claim of the theatre company, which the Folio enforces'. Meres was a schoolmaster and divine, with an interest in literature, but not, as far as we know, in any relations with the players, such as might lead him to act as their catspaw in a commercial fraud. Even if he went to the players for his list, there is no reason to suppose that they told him anything but the truth. The facts must have been well enough known in the London of 1598, and any false claim for Shakespeare would have been open to the challenge of Chapman or another. The testimony of Meres, even if it stood alone, would be at least as good evidence for Shakespeare's authorship of the early plays of the canon as we have for Peele's authorship of *The Arraignment of Paris* in a casual reference by Nashe, or for Kyd's authorship of *The Spanish Tragedy* in a casual reference by Heywood, or for Marlowe's authorship of *Tamburlaine*, of which there is no contemporary record at all. Yet take away these, and Mr. Robertson's whole elaborate edifice of conjectural ascriptions falls to the ground.

I will now leave Mr. Robertson and his Marlowe and Chapman complexes. I turn to the parallel speculations started by Professor Pollard and pursued by Mr. Dover Wilson in his new edition of the plays. Here the problem of the canon is approached from another angle. The emphasis is less upon versification and diction than upon critical bibliography; the study of printing-house usage in handling copy, of the relation which the copy for the plays may have borne to Shakespeare's autograph, of the changes which that copy may have undergone before and after it reached his hands. The methods of critical bibliography are a notable addition to the equipment of scholarship. But scepticism may be permitted as to whether they really carry the superstructure of theory about the revision of the canonical plays, which Mr. Wilson is piling upon them. His work is, of course, only beginning. It has now covered seven of the comedies, and not one of them is allowed to be an integral and untouched product of Shakespeare's creative energy, in the form in which he first conceived and wrought it. Inevitably I throw Mr. Wilson's cautious and modestly expressed hypotheses into more categorical statements. *Comedy of Errors* is 'of Shakespeare's writing in the main', but it is a revision of an older play, perhaps the *Historie of Error* given by a boy company at court in 1577; and of this parts have been retained, including the doggerel, none of which is Shakespeare's. Moreover, the extant text is an abridgement made in the playhouse by two distinct scribes. *Two Gentlemen* is also an abridgement, with passages added by the adapter, who contributed the whole character of Speed. *Love's Labour's Lost* was based by Shakespeare upon a play by a writer of the 'eighties. He himself gave it a revision, and may then have eliminated bits of the original which he at first let stand. Traces of the first Shakespearean version are left, owing to imperfect cancellation in the copy. The Folio text shows some further playhouse alteration. *Much Ado* contains two strata of Shake-spearean work, and has therefore also been revised. There is no obvious indication of a second hand, although an earlier play may have served as a source. Here again there are play-house alterations in the Folio text. *Merry Wives* is a transforma-tion by Shakespeare, 'perhaps, with help from others', of an earlier play, *The Jealous Comedy*, of which parts remain. There may have been an intermediate version. I do not understand Mr. Wilson to regard *The Jealous Comedy* as Shakespeare's own. In *Measure for Measure*, Shakespeare may only have re-cast an old play, with a history going back to Whetstone's *Promos and Cassandra*. But the text, as we have it, has under-gone a double adaptation by later hands; firstly an abridge-ment, secondly an expansion, accompanied by the re-writing of Shakespearean verse-scenes as prose. Finally, *The Tempest* has had a pre-history and a post-history. Substantially, it is a late recast by Shakespeare of an earlier play, perhaps his own, and at this recast, matter originally played in scenes before the wreck has been put into narrative form. Then the recast has itself been abridged, mainly by Shakespeare, and into the abridgement has been inserted the mask, the authorship of which is left undetermined. Mr. Wilson does not, it will be seen, extrude Shakespeare from any of the seven comedies in as wholesale a fashion as that in which Mr. Robertson extrudes him from *Richard II* or *Henry V*. But he finds much alloy due to earlier versions and much alloy due to later adaptations; and these, together with the habit ascribed to Shakespeare of re-vising his own work, produce sufficiently ambiguous results.

Implicit in it all is the doctrine of continuous copy. The foundation of this doctrine has, I think, four corner-stones. The first is a notion of theatrical precaution and economy; pre-caution in not having too many copies of a play about, lest one should fall into the hands of a rival company; economy, in avoiding unnecessary expenditure upon copyist's charges. The second is the actual condition of a particular manuscript which has been preserved, that of *Sir Thomas More*. This has been plausibly shown by Dr. Greg to have been originally written out in a single hand; then altered in several other hands, partly by cancellations and marginal insertions on the original pages, and partly by tearing off some of the original pages and substi-tuting separate slips; then submitted to a censor and marked by him with directions for the modification of disallowed passages;

and finally, or at an earlier stage, gone through by a stage-manager, who added some technical notes for the production. Thirdly, there is the obvious re-writing, scene for scene, of the *Contention of York and Lancaster* as *2* and *3 Henry VI*. And, fourthly, there is the courageous attempt of Professor Pollard and Mr. Wilson themselves to explain the relation of the 'bad' to the 'good' Quartos of certain Shakespearean plays by a theory which entails the progressive revision of lost versions. And so we arrive at the notion of the long-lived manuscript in the tiring-house wardrobe, periodically taken out for a revival and as often worked upon by fresh hands, abridged and expanded, recast to fit the capabilities of new performers, brightened with current topical allusions, written up to date to suit new tastes in poetic diction. Additional scenes may be inserted. If the old pages will no longer hold the new matter, they may be mutilated and replaced by partial transcripts. In the end hardly a single line may remain as it was in the beginning. Yet, in a sense, it is the same play, even as our human bodies, the cellular matter of which is continuously renewed, remain our bodies from the cradle to the grave. A perpetual form; an evanescent ὕλη! Who is the author of such a play? We cannot tell. The soul gets a 'dusty answer', when hot on that particular certainty.

Again I will attempt one or two general propositions bearing upon the issue. I feel some doubt whether the case of *Sir Thomas More* is altogether typical; whether, that is to say, the Master of the Revels would as a rule have been willing to accept for reading a play in the state of picturesque confusion which characterizes that famous document. Professor Pollard, I gather, thinks that he would, and explains it by a reference to 'the easy temper of English officialdom at all periods'. Well, Dr. Pollard is an English official, and so am I, and that is the kind of compliment we bandy between ourselves. Comments in a different tone sometimes drift in to us from the outside world. I am sure, however, that if the Master of the Revels had to tackle many manuscripts like *Sir Thomas More*, that progressive increase in his emoluments, which is a feature in the history of the office during the seventeenth century, was well justified. And personally, I feel that his instinct would have been to call for clean transcripts. Clean transcripts would, of course, be fatal to the doctrine of continuous copy in its extreme form, and in the preparation of them most of the bibliographical evidence, upon which Mr. Wilson relies to prove the revision of plays, would disappear. That any substantial revision, as distinct perhaps from a mere abridgement, would entail a fresh application for the Master's allowance must, I think, be taken for granted. The rule was that his hand must be 'at the latter end of the booke they doe play'; and in London, at least, any company seriously departing from the allowed book would run a considerable risk.[1]

Whether the manuscript of *Sir Thomas More* is typical or not, Mr. Wilson has, of course, no such direct evidence for any play of the canon. He supplies its place by pointing to indications of what he calls 'bibliographical disturbance' in the early editions, departures from typographical uniformity, such as the use for printer's copy of an analogous revised manuscript might explain. There are passages written as blank verse, but set up by the printer as prose. There are incomplete lines of verse, taken by Mr. Wilson as signs of 'cuts'. There are passages which duplicate one another and suggest the accidental survival of alternative versions. There are variations of nomenclature in speech-headings and stage-directions, which may betray composition by different hands or at different dates. It may be observed that, while bibliography can constitute the existence of these phenomena, and can sometimes contribute to an explanation of them from a knowledge of printing-house methods, it can by no means always give a full explanation. And then the bibliographer, like the rest of us, has to fall back upon what he can learn or guess of the methods of the tiring-house, or upon his own insight into literary psychology. Thus the setting up of verse as prose is explained, prettily enough, as due to the failure of compositors to appreciate the metrical character of insertions written continuously in cramped margins. But if you ask why any particular insertion was made, bibliography is dumb. Mr. Wilson tends to guess that it was made as part of a general revision. I find myself often guessing that it was only an after-thought at the time of original writing. Similarly, a broken line may be, and I dare say often is, due to a 'cut', but

---

[1] This raises a further question. Did the Master himself keep copies of allowed books for purposes of control? Certainly Herbert laid down in 1633 that such copies must be furnished to him by the book-keepers, but it is not clear whether he was establishing a new or asserting an old practice. A reference to the burning of Sir George Buck's books suggests the latter. But this also is obscure; it is possible that these were not books kept by Buck, but licensed by him, and burnt at the Fortune in 1621.

it may also be a mere rhythmical variation and it may often indicate a dramatic pause, for reflection or the insertion of stage business. And it is not bibliographical knowledge, but a feeling for rhythm and dramatic values, that must determine the most likely explanation in each case. Mr. Wilson is, of course, just as well qualified to apply the literary as the bibliographical criteria. But the doctrine of continuous copy seems to have a great fascination for him.

I will draw to a close with some 'external' reasons for thinking that the amount of revision in the canon is not likely to be very great. The 'revival' of old plays was familiar to the Elizabethan stage. I first note the technical phrase in a letter of 1605, which states that the King's men had 'revived' *Love's Labour's Lost*. 'Revived' is printed 'revised' by a contributor to Mr. Wilson's edition; that is a mere slip, but revival and revision are not synonymous. The distinction between a new and a revived play has financial implications in Sir Henry Herbert's office notes of 1622–42. In 1628 he secured from the King's men a 'benefit' during each summer and winter, 'to be taken out of the second daye of a revived play'. In 1633 he laid down that 'ould revived playes', as well as 'new' ones, must be brought for allowance, and fixed or confirmed fees of £2 for reading a new play and £1 for an old one. He has a significant entry of the £1 on one occasion, as being for allowance 'to add scenes to an ould play and to give it out for a new one'. After the Restoration, a dispute, of which we have not the conclusion, arose as to whether the Master's fee 'for supervising reviv'd plaies' was of ancient custom, and as to 'how long plaies may be laid asyde, ere he shall judge them to be reviv'd'. All this is late evidence and complicated by Herbert's bureaucratic tendency to magnify his office and multiply his emoluments. But the notions involved were clearly ancient, and even at the Rose a measure of revision probably entitled a 'revived' play to rank as 'new'. When Henslowe marks *Longshanks* in his diary as n.e. we need not suppose that we have to do with anything but a recast of Peele's *Edward I*. There was money in it. Even if the entrance charges for a new play were not higher, novelty had its appeal to the Elizabethan temperament. Dekker and Jonson have their laugh at the poets employed as 'play-patchers' and 'play-dressers'. I dare say the process was often only colourable. 'New titles warrant not a play for new', says a seventeenth-century prologue. On the other hand, a popular stock play, a 'get-penny', might draw well enough at a revival, without revision. Revision then, as well as revival, is a *vera causa* on the Elizabethan stage. It is more difficult to give a quantitative estimate of its frequency. But something can be collected from Henslowe's dealings with the Admiral's men, and something at a later date from Herbert's notes. During the six years from 1597 to 1603 the Admiral's men acquired about 100 new plays, paying fees to the poets which exclude any probability that we have only to do with 'new titles'. Of these we can trace the actual production of about 50, from the purchase for them of new garments and properties; others may, of course, have been furnished from the existing tiring-house stock. As against the 50 new plays, we can trace on similar evidence about 23 revivals. These had probably been exceptionally successful old plays, since 13 of them have come down to us in print, a quite disproportionate number, in view of the oblivion which has overtaken most of the 300 or so plays named by Henslowe. But most of these revivals do not seem to have been accompanied by any substantial payments to poets for carrying out the work. There are ten payments. Three are small sums for 'altering' or 'mending' plays, in one case a new and not a revived one, for the court, presumably as a result of the special scrutiny which plays selected for court performance underwent from the Revels officers. Three others are only for the provision of prologues and epilogues, in one case also for the court. There are, therefore, during these six years and for these 23 revivals, only four cases of substantial revision, carrying substantial fees to the poets.[1] We have three of the four revised plays, and two of them we have both in the revised and the unrevised forms, so that we can see exactly what took place. They are *Doctor Faustus* and *The Spanish Tragedy*; in each case the revision amounted to the insertion of new scenes into an otherwise substantially unaltered text. The third play is *Old Fortunatus*. Here we have only the revised text; the original was probably written in two parts, and the revision compressed them into one. Henslowe's record, therefore, bears very little testimony to any widespread practice of revising plays upon revival. It bears still less to

---

[1] The normal payment for a new play was £6. The revision of *Dr. Faustus* and *Tasso's Melancholy* cost in each case £4; that of *The Spanish Tragedy* £2 and an unspecified part of £10; that of *Old Fortunatus* £9, including some further alterations for the court.

any literary recasting of the whole substance of revived plays, such as the theories which I have sketched envisage. I do not overlook the possible difference in methods between Shakespeare's company and the Admiral's. Two plays belonging to the former, outside the canon, have undergone alteration of known character. One is *The Malcontent*, the other *Mucedorus*; in both the revision took the form of inserting scenes, not of stylistic rehandling. Jonson, no doubt, re-wrote *Every Man in his Humour*, before the folio of 1616, and replaced the work of a collaborator by his own in *Sejanus*, before publication. But Jonson's literary attitude to his 'Works' is too personal to be taken as representative.

I come now to Sir Henry Herbert's notes. Such extracts from these as have been preserved record 130 licences for the production of plays between 1622 and 1642. Only fifteen were old plays, and in only seven is there any record of revision. One is a play of Fletcher's 'corrected' by Shirley; one had undergone 'renewing' and one 'alterations'; four had had one or more scenes added. We cannot be sure that the eighteenth-century scholars took all such notices out of Herbert's office-book, while it was available. And we cannot be sure that the Elizabethans and Jacobeans were not fonder of re-writing plays than the Carolines. But, for what it is worth, Herbert's evidence tends to confirm Henslowe's.

We ought to be very grateful to Mr. Robertson and Mr. Dover Wilson. We had come to think that all the critical questions about Shakespeare were disposed of; the biographical facts and even a little more than the facts chronicled, the canon and the apocrypha fixed, the chronological order determined, the text established; that there was not much left to be done with Shakespeare, except perhaps to read him. They have shown us that it is not so; and we must now go over the ground again, and turn our notional assents, with whatever modifications may prove justified, into real assents. We have all the spring joy of re-digging a well-tilled garden.

1924.

Every age will inevitably refashion the interpretative criticism of Shakespeare to its own mood. But, so far as the bare marshalling of facts is concerned, it must often have seemed, during the long process of the years, as if finality had been reached. Perhaps even Heminges and Condell thought that they had achieved it, when they painfully exhumed from the tiring-house coffers eighteen plays, hitherto unprinted, and furnished authoritative texts to replace the 'stolne and surreptitious copies'—not, indeed, so many as their preface suggested—of others. Here at last were the works of their beloved fellow, 'absolute in their numbers, as he conceived them'. Perhaps the preface might have been longer, if Heminges and Condell had known how many questions about the origin and stage history and chronology of those works the twentieth-century researcher would have liked to put to them. And perhaps it is as well that they did not know, since in that event much of the researcher's entrancing occupation would have been gone. They did not even furnish a biography. Possibly one was written or planned by Thomas Heywood, although no 'fellow' of Shakespeare, among those unfinished and lost *Lives of All the Poets*, for which we would so gladly barter, many times over, his *Gunaikeion* and his *Hierarchy of the Angels*. It is to the piety of a later actor, Thomas Betterton, that we owe most of the facts put together by Nicholas Rowe in the first formal biography of 1709. Presumably Rowe also envisaged finality, although we smile when he says that 'tho' the works of Mr. Shakespear may seem to many not to want a comment, yet I fancy some little account of the man himself may not be thought improper to go along with them'; and Malone pathetically points out how many contemporaries of Shakespeare, still alive in the days of Betterton and Rowe, might have been, but were not, questioned. It is likely that little was garnered by the antiquary William Oldys, sitting there in his room at the Heralds' Office, with sheaves of Shakespearean notes hung in bags around the walls. These notes have vanished. The unreliable George Steevens printed some items of gossip, which may have drifted to Oldys through Pope at the Earl of Oxford's table. Sir Sidney Lee says that the originals of these are extant in some *Adversaria* by Oldys 'now in the British Museum'. But I have searched for them there in vain. It is ironical that Oldys did not even discover the record of the Shakespeare arms, which lay at the Heralds' Office all the time.

Then at the end of the century came Malone himself, a very competent scholar for his time, unwearied both in archival research and in personal inquiries up and down Warwickshire. He opened up the documents at Stratford and Dulwich College and the Record Office, trounced the Ireland forgeries, and made a big contribution both to the chronological and textual history of the plays and to the biography of the playwright. We must always remain grateful to Malone. His results, taking their latest posthumous form in the *Third Variorum Shakespeare* of 1821, once more looked like finality, and his authority remained great during the first half of the nineteenth century. Something was added by Collier, while darkening counsel with new forgeries, by Joseph Hunter, by George Russell French, and much by J. O. Halliwell-Phillipps. These in their turn led up in the later Victorian days to a vast outburst of concurrent activities; the textual work of Clark and Wright, the spiritual biography of Edward Dowden, the *Quellenforschung* of the Germans, the stimulating but airy speculations of F. G. Fleay, the corporate studies of F. J. Furnivall and his colleagues of the New Shakspere Society, culminating in the great series of Quarto Facsimiles. A new synthesis was required, and has been provided by Clark and Wright's Cambridge text, by Sir Sidney Lee's *Life*, gradually developing from 1898 to 1925 out of an article for the *Dictionary of National Biography*, by the recently completed Arden edition, and by the illustrative learning of *Shakespeare's England*. Here is a ripe harvest gathered into the barns.

And even now the questioning spirit of man is not satisfied. Industrious students are still searching for fresh information, delving into foundations, challenging presuppositions, endeavouring to work out new methods of investigation. Thus is a spirit of unrest abroad, a conviction that nowhere yet has the last word been said, that there remain undiscovered secrets in the plays which a renewed probing of texts and records may reveal. This is as it should be. A scholarship which merely accepts is bound to become sterile. It is worth while, therefore, to make some survey of the position, to indicate what lines of development are being pursued, and perhaps to speculate as to where the possibilities of advance seem greatest.

I think it is doubtful whether much is to be expected in the way of new external facts of biography. Halliwell-Phillipps is said to have hoped to the end for a discovery of papers belonging to Shakespeare, which might have been taken by his granddaughter into the household of the Barnards of Abington and dispersed at the break-up of that household. The chances are that any such papers have long ago fed the flames. No doubt some mouldering garret in some English manor-house might still yield up a treasure, but such things lie on the knees of the gods, and are hardly to be obtained by prayer, sacrifice, or research. The wooden frame of a horn-book has just been found in Anne Hathaway's cottage at Shottery. On it are roughly cut the initials W. S., or perhaps W. B. If it is S, it is not much like the S of Shakespeare's script. And although Shakespeare married young, he was not quite young enough to take his horn-book with him when he went a-wooing to Anne Hathaway (if it was Anne Hathaway) at Shottery (if it was at Shottery). In any event, the *trouvaille* is for sentiment, rather than for erudition. The most it could tell us is that Shakespeare once used a horn-book, and that we could have taken for granted. Perhaps there might be something to be learnt from a more systematic examination than has yet been undertaken of the parochial documents of St. Saviour's, Southwark, and other London churches, or of the registers of the ecclesiastical jurisdictions. And one has a haunting feeling that the well-preserved Corporation archives of London ought to contain some more continuous records of the civic licensing of playing companies and playhouses, comparable to those of the Mayor's Court at Norwich, than have yet come to light through the repertories and journals and collections of correspondence. Anything from these sources, no doubt, might be expected to bear rather upon the theatrical environment than upon the personality of Shakespeare. There are also unexplored recesses of the Record Office, and in particular the uncalendared pleadings, depositions, and judgments arising out of lawsuits in the High Courts. Here the industrious researcher, at the expense of many unproductive days and with no Ariadne's clue except a handful of likely names to guide him, might hope to come upon something new, since Elizabethan actors were always a litigious folk. It was, indeed, from judicial records and by some such method that the latest biographical contributions of importance were made by Professor Wallace, of Nebraska. A group of lawsuits yielded valuable information on the nature of Shakespeare's financial interests in the Globe and Blackfriars Theatres, and another disclosed the poet as a lodger in a family of Huguenot tire-makers, where he helped the course of true love to run smooth for a daughter of the household and her father's apprentice.

The plays, however, rather than the biography, are the main preoccupation of the twentieth-century researcher, who approaches them with an open mind and a laudable determination not to take for granted the conclusions of his predecessors. It is only reasonable to expect that, in any age in which minute critical attention is paid to a body of bygone literature, theories will emerge which a conservative instinct is tempted promptly to brand as heresies. Any such summary formula of dismissal runs a risk of proving unjust. Heresy and the reaction against heresy and the search for a reconciliation have always been the dialectical process by which knowledge has advanced its frontiers and consolidated its territory. Certainly there are revolutionary notions abroad about the authenticity and homogeneity of the Shakespearean canon, as handed down in the First Folio and the independent Quartos. Against its authenticity it is claimed that to a large extent the plays, or many of them, are not Shakespeare's handiwork at all; against its homogeneity that, in so far as they are Shakespeare's, they often represent, in the form in which we have them, his later recensions of his original compositions. The more perturbing scepticism, to the conservative instinct, is naturally that which challenges authenticity. I do not suppose that many students go all the way with Mr. Oliphant, who finds Shakespeare's matter much overlaid by Massinger's in *The Tempest* and in *Cymbeline*, or with Mr. Robertson, who substantially transfers *Romeo and Juliet*, *Richard II*, *Henry V*, *Julius Caesar*, and *The Comedy of Errors* to Christopher Marlowe, *The Two Gentlemen of Verona* to Robert Greene, and *Troilus and Cressida*, *All's Well That Ends Well*, and *Measure for Measure* to George Chapman. But these are only extreme examples of a very general hesitation to accept as equally Shakespeare's all the different manners of writing verse or prose and all the different degrees of poetic merit which the plays of the canon exhibit.

The sceptics start, as a rule, from subjective judgements of style. And these, although one may sometimes suspect them to be based on too exclusive an attention to the best work of an unequal writer, are fundamental and hardly to be affected by argument. One can only plead for caution, in view of the very considerable difficulties which beset the discrimination of styles, especially where one hand is supposed to have over-written the lines of another. The development of Shakespeare's maturing style, in its most characteristic manifestations, has been traced with some success. It is not so easy to establish a criterion which will distinguish its less characteristic manifestations from the maturing styles of his contemporaries. And it is still less easy to disentangle his immature style from that of the school of poets which made an environment for his novitiate. It is, I think, justifiable to speak of these poets—Marlowe, Peele, Greene, Lodge, Nashe, Kyd, and others more dimly discerned—as a school. They worked in collaboration and interchanged their praises. They have a common bond in classical knowledge and the attempt to conquer the popular stage for literature. They owe a common debt to Seneca and his English court imitators. And they largely share a common style, which derives its stores of diction, phrasing, and imagery, from the Senecans, from Spenser, and from the Elizabethan translators of Latin poets. Marlowe dominates, with a genius and a feeling for beauty beyond that of his fellows. Kyd, the 'grammarian', stands a little aloof, but the influence of his rhetoric is pervasive. I do not suggest that they all handled the common style in exactly the same fashion. No doubt each man wore his rue with a difference. And if we had a sufficient body of undisputed dramatic work from each, we might determine the various ways in which the common elements were combined and modified, and get a clear conception of dramatic personalities, which in its turn would enable us to estimate the affinities of the young Shakespeare, and to watch his emancipation from the bonds of the school. Unfortunately the available material is extremely scanty. The number of plays which there is external evidence for assigning to any one writer only ranges from two to seven, and the evidential value of some of these is small, because they are only preserved in hopelessly corrupt texts or are complicated by an indefinite amount of collaboration. The style of non-dramatic work can be compared; the translations of Marlowe, the pamphlets of Greene, the ceremonial poems of Peele. But these only give limited help in judging the handling of dialogued verse. Probably each writer is further represented by some of the many anonymous plays of the period, although there were other prolific dramatists, such as Thomas Watson, whose work is unknown and who may be responsible for some of these. It is only through the accidental allusions of contemporaries that we can ascribe the anonymous *Tamburlaine* to Marlowe and the anonymous *Spanish Tragedy* to Kyd. Many attempts have been made to pick out other masterless plays and to claim them on internal evidence for this or that known writer. Parallels of vocabulary, of syntax, of the collocation of words, of metaphor and simile, of dramatic motive, are carefully collected. Enthusiasm for a discovery sometimes tends to outrun caution. Points of similarity are stressed. Others, no less important, of difference are often disregarded. Then the play so appropriated is made itself to contribute to a further induction, designed to cast the net wider and to bring in yet other plays or parts of plays. Kyd and Peele have been the chief beneficiaries of this reasoning. Obviously it grows weaker as it extends its scope. In its earlier stages it is seductive, but, like other applications of the unchecked method of agreement, far from convincing. Logically it should have been preceded by a comprehensive preliminary investigation, directed to showing what stylistic features belong to the common stock and what may properly be regarded as characteristic of an individual. And parallels, even if well established, are double-edged weapons. No doubt constant writers tend to echo themselves. But so, too, do the members of a school tend to echo each other; and in particular, as a school acquires disciples, these tend to echo their masters. It is often more a matter of subconscious reminiscence than of purposed imitation. 'Half echoes' was a happy term coined by Rupert Brooke for such a literary give and take. Perhaps it is not a paradox to say that, the more obvious a parallel is, the less testimony it bears to identity of authorship. Little habitual mannerisms of phrase, which might readily pass unnoticed, are safer guides than reproductions of impressive thoughts or images. Mere words pass like coins from hand to hand. And where, as is rarely the case, an actual borrowing of one or more complete lines seems unmistakable, it surely points to anything rather than a single author. It may be deliberate plagiarism, since discipleship is not always either discreet or honest. It may be the trick of a reporter's memory, bringing alien matter into a

speech which he is trying to reproduce. It may be burlesque.
Thus in *The Spanish Tragedy* Kyd writes:

> And if the world like not this tragedy,
> Hard is the hap of old Hieronimo.

And after the play-scene, Hamlet exclaims:

> For if the King like not the comedy,
> Why then, belike, he likes it not, perdy.

It is simple to treat this, with Mr. Robertson and others, as
evidence for Kyd's hand in *Hamlet*. Shakespeare had smiled,
as we smile, over the bathos of *The Spanish Tragedy*, and makes
the overwrought Hamlet find utterance for his pent-up excite-
ment, characteristically enough, in a literary parody. The
manner of Shakespeare when he wrote *Hamlet* is of course far
more recognizable than his manner, or that of any other dramatist, a decade before. The analysis of style must go a great
deal further before it is possible to lay a finger on any passage
of a play of the early 'nineties and say with confidence, 'This
is Marlowe', or 'This is Greene', or 'This is the young
Shakespeare'.

There is at present a more hopeful field in the activities of
the so-called 'bibliographical' school of researchers. These are
not so completely detached from literary considerations as some
of the exponents of the school, perhaps ironically, profess. But
at least they approach their problem from the bibliographical
angle, beginning with a close investigation of the typographical
features of the old prints and an attempt to deduce from these
the way in which the plays were composed and the nature of
the 'copy' furnished to the printers. The method has been
hailed as a revolution through which for the first time 'the door
of Shakespeare's workshop stands ajar'. A modest qualification
is necessary. Scholarship has its continuity and leaves little
room for revolutionaries. Many of the typographical peculiarities, which are now much under discussion, were noted, if not
always rightly interpreted, by the versatile Mr. Fleay; and,
although some editors have erroneously supposed that the First
Folio represents the final form in which Shakespeare desired his
plays to stand, the superior authority of many of the Quartos,
which is a cardinal principle of the bibliographers, has always
been proclaimed by the soundest students, from Malone to Mr.
P. A. Daniel and his fellow workers on the Quarto facsimiles.
But certainly the new school comes to its task with a better

equipment than its predecessors. It is familiar with the history of printing, with the organization of Elizabethan printing-houses, and with the operations of the Stationers' Company and the press censors. It has studied the technical processes of the printer's workshop and the psychology of the compositor. It is accustomed to think in terms of type and paper, and can distinguish between textual errors which may reasonably be attributed to the craftsmen and those for which some other explanation must be found.

Its first scientific achievement was the detection of a group of Quartos, bearing various dates, but all in fact printed in 1619, and apparently representing an abortive attempt at a collected edition of Shakespearean plays, some years in advance of the First Folio. Incidentally, questions of priority between the Quartos both of *A Midsummer-Night's Dream* and of *The Merchant of Venice* were finally settled. This was bibliography pure and simple. The lead in the enterprise was taken by Dr. A. W. Pollard, of the British Museum, although much was also done by Dr. W. W. Greg, and the clinching stroke was reserved for a transatlantic scholar. It is to Dr. Pollard that the school looks as its founder. He is not only one of the most accomplished of living bibliographers, but also a critic, an acknowledged Chaucerian expert, an editor of Sidney and Herrick and much else. Of all men he is the least entitled to waive his claim to a literary as well as a bibliographical judgement. His optimism and accessibility to new ideas have struck the temperamental notes for the whole movement. He is even an optimist about the honesty of Elizabethan publishers and the desire and ability of Elizabethan printers, at any rate in their more sober moments, to give a faithful rendering of the copy set before them. Naturally, therefore, he has a good opinion of the soundness of the extant Shakespearean texts, and this he has done much to justify by establishing from the condition of surviving dramatic manuscripts the use of author's copy as prompt copy for the actors, thus countering the older notion of the constant intervention of playhouse transcribers, and giving plausibility to the conclusion that some at least of the Quartos may have been set up direct from Shakespeare's own papers. His *Shakespeare's Folios and Quartos* and his *Shakespeare's Fight with the Pirates*, both full of reasonableness and learning, are fundamental treatises for the modern researcher. Optimism perhaps confers the faculty of seeing rather more in a dark room than is apparent to the ordinary eye. Dr. Pollard, while maintaining the authority of the 'Good' Quartos and limiting the applicability of Heminges and Condell's derogatory epithet 'surreptitious' to the half-dozen admittedly corrupt texts which he calls the 'Bad' Quartos, at least shares the responsibility for a highly speculative theory as to the origin of the latter. This conceives them to be based upon versions of pre-Shakespearean plays, partly revised by Shakespeare, then shortened for provincial performance, and finally contaminated by additions taken from more fully revised Shakespearean versions, which had supplanted them on the London stage. It is a highly ingenious conjecture, but it raises considerable difficulties and entails several assumptions on points of provincial theatrical practice about which our ignorance is profound.

In handling another problem, palaeography has come to the aid of bibliography. If learning can ever be sensational, it was sensational in the revival by Sir Edward Maunde Thompson of the suggestion, tentatively put forward many years ago, that certain leaves in the manuscript of *Sir Thomas More*, which contain a scene of London riot and a long speech of Sir Thomas to the rioters, may be written in Shakespeare's hand, and the lines, therefore, presumably of his composition. Sir Edward Maunde Thompson's authority as a veteran student of penmanship is unrivalled, and the pages in his *Shakespeare's Handwriting* and in *Shakespeare's Hand in Sir Thomas More*, which, with the aid of numerous facsimiles, expound his theory, make fascinating reading. Here the formation and linking of the letters in the fragment, each in its turn, is compared in minute detail with those in the half-dozen indubitable specimens of Shakespeare's script which have come down to us. Admittedly the basis for an induction is slight. With the exception of the words 'By me', which preface one of them, the indubitable scripts are limited to signatures, and it is the unfortunate habit of mankind to frame its signatures somewhat differently from its straightforward texts. On these and other grounds Sir Edward's findings have had to face searching criticisms from fellow-palaeographers, notably from Dr. S. A. Tannenbaum, of New York, which seem to a layman to require more answer than they have yet received. The date of the fragment and the literary quality of the lines have also been matter for much controversy; and critics remain divided as to whether the composition is likely to be Shakespeare's. It will not be inconsistent

with what has been said as to the difficulty of style-discrimina-
tion, where work not the most characteristic is concerned, if I
venture to express the personal opinion that it may be, rather
than must be, his. If Sir Edward's belief is accepted, some
rather interesting inferences follow. Shakespeare would appear
to have written rapidly and with many contractions, to have
corrected himself more frequently than we should gather from
what Heminges and Condell say about the absence of 'blots'
from his papers, and to have been very summary in his indication of the names of speakers. The passage also shows certain
abnormalities of spelling, analogies to which have been traced
in some of the Quartos, and have confirmed the impression that
Shakespearean manuscripts may underlie these. No doubt, if
we could be sure that we knew how Shakespeare formed his
letters and knew what his habits of spelling were, the knowledge would be a valuable instrument for the solution of textual
cruces.

The validity of Sir Edward Maunde Thompson's contention
is assumed for all practical purposes by Professor Dover Wilson, the textual editor who co-operates with Sir Arthur Quiller-
Couch in the new Cambridge series of the plays. This edition
has now reached its tenth volume, and each so far has been full
of freshness and stimulus, however much one may dissent from
its concrete conclusions. Here is no hidebound or sterile
scholarship; no mere restating of well-worn themes. Professor
Wilson is the romantic of the bibliographical movement. Research is for him a delightful and inexhaustible adventure of
the mind. His acute observation revels in the detection of
irregular stage-directions, speech-prefixes, and catchwords, in
the evidence for 'cuts' and interpolations to be drawn from
broken or misdivided lines, and from other disturbances of the
text. His vivid imagination leaps ahead to the most ingenious
of explanatory hypotheses. Sometimes, I fear, it plays fantastic
tricks before high heaven. In the outcome we are furnished
with elaborate reconstructions of the textual history of play
after play, often involving the building up of copy for the
printers from actors' 'parts', often the rehandling by Shakespeare of his original work, or the incorporation of pre-Shakespearean or post-Shakespearean matter. Herein Professor
Wilson, from a different angle, approaches the standpoint of
Mr. Robertson. No doubt they would generally repudiate each
other's specific interpretations. But at least they share the

dominating conception of a standing stage text, preserved as a valuable possession in the tiring-room, transferred, it may be from company to company, remodelled and written up to date in accordance with shifting standards of taste, by dramatist after dramatist, but preserving some kind of continuous life and bearing to the end some traces of its successive reincarnations. The manuscript may undergo transcription, if the interests of legibility make transcription imperative; or it may remain as a conglomerate in which the original text shows dimly through a mass of deletions and interlineations and marginal insertions and bits of new dialogue written on attached slips of paper. It is easy to see how such a conception is derived, on the one hand from Dr. Pollard's doctrine of the use of author's manuscript as stage copy, and on the other from the actual condition of the *Sir Thomas More* text. But it is certainly perturbing to the literary mind; for who can be said to be the author of such a play, and how is such a genesis reconcilable with the internal evidence which Shakespeare's plays at least seem to carry, for all their offhandedness and inconsequences, of a ruling idea or sentiment in each, due to the unifying power of a shaping spirit of imagination? The Hebrew Scriptures, and possibly, if Professor Gilbert Murray is right, even the Greek epics, may have come into existence through some such process of secular accretion. But surely the Elizabethan poets had the tradition of conscious artists before them. I do not think that either Mr. Robertson or Professor Wilson has ever quite fairly faced this problem. Mr. Robertson, at least, seems contemptuous of any notion of dramatic art which makes it more than the writing of dull or inspired sections of dialogue.

It is easy to exaggerate the evidence for a prevalent practice of revision in the Elizabethan playhouses. Certainly the actors cut and interpolated the author's texts. They put in bits of irrelevant *spectacle* and comic gag for the clowns. There was some adaptation as between public and court or other private performances. And there was some shortening, for reasons that remain rather obscure. Possibly the use of daylight theatres entailed shorter representations in the winter than in the summer. Occasionally, also, a popular old play was altered to give it a new lease of life. But in the clear cases this was a matter of putting in a few new scenes rather than of complete stylistic revision. Wilmot's revision of *Gismond of Salerne* and Jonson's of *Every Man in his Humour* are exceptions which prove the rule, for they may be ascribed, the first with certainty and the second with probability, to literary and not theatrical motives. When a play was dead, its plot might become the basis for a new play. *The Taming of the Shrew*, *King John*, and *King Lear* had such an origin. They may be none the better for it, but they are substantially new plays, and not revisions of old plays. *Lear* at least Shakespeare fashioned to his own dramatic purposes, as he chose. He turned it from a tragicomedy into a tragedy. Beyond this use of old plots there is not much evidence, other than such as Professor Wilson can get out of textual disturbances or Mr. Robertson out of variations in style, for Shakespeare as a reviser either of Shakespeare or of any one else. Several of the plays exist in longer and shorter versions. As a rule it is demonstrable that the longer version was the original, and that it was afterwards shortened. Shakespeare's pen flowed freely, and the actors had to reduce him within time-limits, at a sacrifice sometimes of dramatic values and often of excellent poetry. The doctrine, repeated from text-book to text-book, of his apprenticeship spent in patching the plays of other men is based partly on Ravenscroft's late seventeenth-century tradition of the 'master touches' he gave to *Titus Andronicus*, partly on Greene's notorious attack on 'Shake-scene', which does not really require any such explanation, but mainly on the long-held belief that the second and third parts of *Henry VI* represent a stylistic revision of *The Contention of York and Lancaster*. It is much more likely that *The Contention* is a corrupt and reported version of a shortened *Henry VI*.

This leads up to the work of yet another representative of the modern spirit, the penetrating and cautious Dr. Greg. Palaeographer as well as bibliographer, Dr. Greg has done yeoman's service to dramatic history by his editions of the Dulwich papers and the Malone Society reprints. It was his masterly transcript of *Sir Thomas More* for the Malone series which focused attention upon that debatable document. His broad grasp of complicated facts and power of remorseless analysis are useful correctives to some of the extravagances of current theorizing. But Dr. Greg, too, is among the pioneers. He has given special attention to the problem of corrupt and shortened texts. In an edition of the 'Bad' Quarto of *The Merry Wives of Windsor* he came to the conclusion that the copy was supplied to the printers by a knavish actor, who had taken the

part of the Host, was able to reproduce his own lines with fai
accuracy, and had obtained sufficient knowledge of the rest o
the play to 'report' it in a bungled form and with many mutila
tions and lapses of memory. In a more recent treatise on *Tw*
Elizabethan Stage Abridgements Dr. Greg takes the similarl
garbled print of Greene's *Orlando Furioso* as the occasion for ;
luminous survey of the whole theory of reporting as the origir
of surreptitious texts. Earlier speculations had generally postu
lated the use of some primitive system of shorthand, and ther
is evidence for the employment of such a method about 1605
But it is doubtful whether any adequate system was availabl
in the sixteenth century, and Dr. Greg has been successful i1
demonstrating that a far from word-perfect and often roughl
summarized memorization by actors is sufficient to explair
most of the peculiarities which surreptitious prints exhibit. H
has been led, he tells us, 'to doubt whether any limit can be se
to the possible perversion which a text may suffer at the hand
of a reporter'. To him must be credited one of the most solic
results of the renewed activity in Shakespearean research. An(
with him this survey may fitly end.

1927.

WILLIAM SHAKESPEARE: AN EPILOGUE

THE study here presented is based upon a lecture which I was privileged to give before the members of the English School at Oxford. A critical eye will probably detect in its closing passages an element of biographical fantasy alien to the strict canons of scholarship. So be it! Where historical evidence fails, we cannot always help, in our old age, dreaming a little about Shakespeare.

My train of thought was started by some remarks of Dr. Granville-Barker, in exposition of a thesis that the last thirty years of work on Shakespeare, have brought about a notable 'transvaluation of values', as a result of which we must regard his plays rather as material for stage-representation than as literature to be read by the fireside. 'The student's approach to Shakespeare', on this view, 'will be something like a *contemporary* approach. He will try to make himself one with the audience at the Globe or Blackfriars.' True, there may be 'certain innate qualities' in the plays which have enabled them to survive their age and the circumstances of their production, and this also, it is admitted, is worth looking into.[1]

The theatre, says Dr. Granville-Barker, when Shakespeare came to it 'was dominated by its actors', who had 'made' it not 'correct', as an academic dramatist might wish it, but an 'exciting place' of 'vigour, unruly passion, and abounding vitality'. Here Shakespeare created 'a new art of acting', aiming at the seemingly spontaneous expression of character in action, which is 'the end of all drama'. If, as perhaps in *Romeo and Juliet*, the characters would not come alive, he could fall back upon a convention, a formula. 'It is a thing the actor understands, and *you can trust him to do the rest*.'[2] Dr. Granville-Barker returns to this theme in his illuminating study of *Hamlet*.[3] Here stage-presentation becomes frankly a 'collaboration' between the dramatist and the actor.

The actor does not lose himself in the character he plays. On the contrary. He not only presents it under his own aspect, he lends it his own

---

1 Preface to *A Companion to Shakespeare Studies* (1934), signed by H. Granville-Barker and G. B. Harrison.

2 *Companion*, 46, 51, 53.

3 *Prefaces to Shakespeare*, Third Series (1937), 3, 5.

emotions too, and he must re-pass the thought of which it is built through the sieve of his own mind. He dissects it and then reconstructs it in terms of his own personality.

Literary dramatists, from Elizabethan days onwards, have been unwilling to recognize this, and have failed accordingly. They would make of the actor a mere mouthpiece. 'To provide raw material for acting', asks Dr. Granville-Barker, 'is there something undignified about it?' We know Ben Jonson's answer. 'Come leave the loathed stage!' he growled. I wish I knew what Shakespeare's would have been.

So far I have been mainly quoting. There is much truth in what Dr. Granville-Barker says. But it is difficult for an Oxford man, who approaches drama from the angles of Aristotle and Bradley, to accept the definition of it as 'the expression of character in action', as the whole truth. He has learnt to regard tragedy as primarily an emotional reaction to the issues of life, and comedy as primarily an intellectual comment on the conduct of life, and the action and speech of a play, not as an end in itself, but as only an instrument for the expression of these. He may or may not think that the impersonations of living mimes intrude more between him and these themes than the masked performances of the Greek stage would have done, but at any rate he feels that a leisurely contemplation by his fireside often illuminates the intention of the dramatist more fully than is possible during the swift progress of a play upon the boards.

It must be added that we are not quite sure what the method of acting on the Elizabethan stage was. The question has recently been raised by Mr. Alfred Harbage, who distinguishes between 'formal' and 'natural' acting, and believes that Elizabethan acting was formal, with little of what is called 'business', and content to evoke its dramatic illusion by conventional movement and gesture, with occasional heightened delivery.[1] I do not know that we have material for deciding the point, since all contemporary criticisms of acting must be relative to existing standards. Thomas Heywood, about 1608, bids a scholar learn how to speak through the practice of acting so that he may 'neither buffet his desk like a mad man, nor stand in his place like a liveless image, demurely plodding, and without any smooth and formal motion'.[2] But 'formal' is a word with many shades of meaning, and we cannot be sure what

[1] 'Elizabethan Acting' (1939, *P.M.L.A.* LIV. 685).
[2] *An Apology for Actors* (1612), 28–9.

significance Heywood attached to it. To use it in Mr. Harbage's sense would perhaps be inconsistent with Heywood's deprecation of standing like a lifeless image. But in any case, Heywood is thinking of academic, not professional, acting. One J. Cocke, about 1615, deprecates *A Common Player*, who 'when he doth hold conference upon the stage; and should look directly in his fellow's face; hee turns about his voice into the assembly for applause-sake, like a Trumpeter in the fields, that shifts places to get an eccho'.[1] John Webster, about the same time, characterizes *An Excellent Player*: 'Nature is often seene in the same scaene with him, but neither on Stilts nor Crutches'; and again, 'What we see him personate, we thinke truely done before us.'[2] Richard Flecknoe describes Burbadge as 'wholly transforming himself into his Part', and 'never falling in his Part when he had done speaking; but with his looks and gesture, maintaining it still unto the heighth'.[3] But Flecknoe was writing in 1664, and may never have seen Burbadge. I do not think that these passages do much to bear out Mr. Harbage's contention. Perhaps his strongest bit of evidence is in the preface to *The Cyprian Conqueror*, extant in a mid-seventeenth century manuscript, but still unprinted.[4]

The other parts of action is in yᵉ gesture, wᶜʰ must be various, as required; as in a sorrowful parte, yᵉ head must hang downe; in a proud, yᵉ head must bee lofty; in an amorous, closed eies, hanging downe lookes, & crossed armes, in a hastie, fumeing, & scratching yᵉ head, &c.

This is certainly 'formal' enough. I have never seen *The Cyprian Conqueror*, but Mr. Harbage says that there is no proof that the author was familiar with the popular stage. Perhaps it was a school play. It is likely enough that, even on the London stage, the early boy companies were trained to act with very conventional gestures. But I have an impression—it can be no more—that during Shakespeare's lifetime the acting by men was becoming more and more 'natural' and realistic, although, of course, both blank verse and the use of boys to take women's parts must always have imposed some limits on the process. Shakespeare himself, in or about 1600, was evidently much occupied with problems of histrionic method in those scenes with the players in *Hamlet*, which, while throwing light on Hamlet's temperament and furnishing a relief to the tenseness of the drama, perhaps do so at rather unnecessary

[1] *Elizabethan Stage*, IV. 255.   [2] Ibid., IV. 258.
[3] Ibid., IV. 370.   [4] *Sloane MS.* 3709.

length. And I think that Hamlet's criticisms, too familiar to quote here, point to the prevalence of a realism sometimes rather overdone.[1]

I find another difficulty in the way of making myself one with the audience at the Globe or Blackfriars. How much of the plays, as Shakespeare wrote them, should I hear? I fall back upon the valuable statistical researches of Mr. Alfred Hart,[2] who has calculated, on a better basis than mine in *The Elizabethan Stage*, the total number of verse-lines and prose equivalents in each of Shakespeare's plays. They range from the 1,753 lines of *The Comedy of Errors* to the 3,762 of *Hamlet*. The average length is about 2,750 lines. It would have been higher, had not several of the plays first printed in the First Folio, notably *Macbeth*, come to us only in cut versions. In all, eleven plays exceed 3,000 lines. Then Mr. Hart extended his investigation to other contemporary plays. The critical period is 1594–1616.

Thirty-three known authors contributed 179 plays in all. Jonson wrote eleven of these, averaging 3,580 lines a play, Shakespeare thirty-two, averaging 2,744 lines. The remaining thirty-one dramatists provided 136 plays that average 2,430 lines.

I am not sure that an average is of very great value where the range is from below 1,600 lines to over 3,000. It is noteworthy that this upper limit is only reached by seven plays besides Shakespeare's and Jonson's.

It is in 1594 that we first get any clear indication of the time available for playing during the period of Shakespeare's activity in a letter of 8 October from Lord Chamberlain Hunsdon to the Lord Mayor, which undertakes that his company, who formerly began to play about 4 p.m., will now begin at two, and have done between four and five.[3] On the face of it this only refers to one company and to 'this winter time'. But it probably represents a general compromise, arrived at after a long period of controversy, and we have no reason to suppose that, apart from inhibitions for plague and the like, it was departed from during Shakespeare's lifetime, so far as the adult companies were concerned. Conceivably, however, the time allowed may have been a little longer during the lighter even-

---

[1] *Hamlet*, II. ii. 577–92; III. ii. 1–50, 262–4.

[2] *R.E.S.* VIII. (1932), 19, 139, 395; X. (1934), 1, reprinted, except the first, in *Shakespeare and the Homilies* (1934).

[3] *Elizabethan Stage*, IV. 316.

ing hours of full summer. On the other hand, the boys of
Paul's only played for two hours about 1601.[1] At any rate,
when Thomas Platter visited London during September and
October 1599, he found plays beginning at 2 p.m.[2] He does
not say when they ended. But he does note that the plays he
saw were followed by dances, and that there were intervals
during which food and drink were brought round. It does not
look as if more than two hours, or at most two hours and a half,
would be available for the main performance. And, in fact, a
number of passages in prologues and the like speak of two
hours as the normal time taken by a play. They begin with the
reference in the Quarto of *Romeo and Juliet* (1597) to 'the two
hours' traffic of our stage', and go on to 1613 at least. Most
of them are in verse, and perhaps should not be taken too
literally, since it would be difficult to get 'two hours and a half'
into a verse line.[3] But at any rate they cannot be stretched to
mean 'three hours'. An exception is the epilogue to Dekker's
If it be Not Good, the Devil is in It (2,700 lines), which records
'three hours of mirth'.

In prose, the induction to Beaumont and Fletcher's *Four
Plays in One* (2,345 lines) promises a King 'that Reigns his
two hours'. It may be a play for boys. That to Jonson's
Bartholomew Fair (4,344 lines) asks 'two houres and an halfe,
and somewhat more'. Dekker, in his *Raven's Almanack*, not a
play, is ironical on an actor who 'shall be glad to play three
houres for two pence to the basest stinkard in London'. Mr.
Hart, after considering this evidence, thinks that the limit of
two hours was rather strictly adhered to. I should myself be
inclined to put it at two hours and a half, which is in fact the
time ascribed to Shakespeare's historical plays in Dryden's
Essay on Dramatic Poesy (1668). Platter's evidence suggests
that this included intervals and sometimes at least a jig, although the latter may not have been invariable.

The unwearied Mr. Hart then proceeded to consider how
fast dramatic blank verse could be given on the stage. He
found that he could read it, without pauses, at the rate of 22
lines a minute, which amounts to 2,640 lines in two hours.

---

[1] *Elizabethan Stage*, II. 21.   [2] *Ibid.*, II. 364.
[3] *Romeo and Juliet* (1597); Dekker, *Whore of Babylon* (1605–7); Barry,
Ram Alley (1607–8); Jonson, *Alchemist* (1610); *Henry VIII* (1612–13); *Two
Noble Kinsmen* (1613); Tailor, *Hog Hath Lost His Pearl* (1613). Cf. Hart,
Shakespeare and the Homilies, 97 sqq.

Allowing ten minutes for pauses in utterance and 'business', he reduced this to 2,420 lines, which comes very near his average of 2,430 lines. Again one must emphasize the dangers of an average to which few individual plays defer. Through the kindness of Dr. Granville-Barker and Mr. Lewis Casson, I was able to obtain some figures from Mr. Casson's recent production of *King Lear* at the Old Vic. Mr. Casson reads continuous blank verse faster than Mr. Hart does, at the rate of about 30 lines a minute. This he would slow down for acting, pauses, processions, and general movement to something like 20 lines for tragedy and 25 for comedy. On this basis he had expected his acting text of 3,071 lines to take just about two and a half hours in performance. In fact, it took three hours and eleven minutes, at an average rate of little over 16 lines a minute. Incidentally, this comes very near the rough estimate of a thousand lines an hour which I made in the *Elizabethan Stage*. No doubt, however, it is true, as Mr. Casson says, that the speech of modern actors is not as 'tripping' as that of Elizabethan ones, and also that the Old Vic is a bad theatre for speech. I may add that, on 'an unassailable authority' cited by Professor Schücking, the performance, without act-intervals, also at the Old Vic, of the full *Hamlet* of 3,762 lines, took four hours and twenty-two minutes.[1]

What are the inferences? First, I think, that, in spite of the prologues, it is safer to regard two hours and a half than two hours as the normal time for a play during 1594–1616; and secondly, that the full texts of Shakespeare's longest plays, as we have them, including at least the eleven plays of over 3,000 lines, were no more likely than Ben Jonson's to have been actually presented at the Globe or Blackfriars. It remains arguable, I suppose, that longer performances were given at court. I do not think it very likely, but here we have very little to go upon. Court entertainments sometimes began at 10 p.m., and sometimes lasted to 1 a.m. or even 2 a.m.[2] But we cannot assume that the whole of those long periods were devoted solely to continuous plays. Music, dancing, a banquet, have all to be thought of. Failing this possible loophole, are we to infer that Shakespeare, like Jonson, wrote for publication, and let the players, in the meantime, do their worst? In the case of Jonson we are not surprised. He was a scholar, and liked to emulate

[1] *Spectator* (15 Oct. 1937).
[2] *Elizabethan Stage*, i. 161, 162, 225.

the ancients. He edited his own plays, or some of them, and called them his *Works*. But Shakespeare, obviously, did nothing of the kind. For whom, then, did he write? For himself? It follows, if this is so, that we must to some extent qualify Dr. Granville-Barker's view of the plays as 'raw material for acting'. And perhaps, after all, we may have to resort to our firesides when we wish to capture the full significance of their tragic or comic intention.

Shakespeare, we know, was in his early London life an actor, a 'Shake-scene', and Henry Chettle, wishing to be apologetic, describes him as 'exelent in the qualitie he professes'. Later references make it doubtful whether he was ever a great actor. John Davies, in 1610, says that he had played 'Kingly parts'. Long after his death, John Aubrey was told that he 'did act exceedingly well', but James Wright that he 'was a much better Poet than Player'. Nicholas Rowe could only learn that 'the Top of his performance was the Ghost in his own *Hamlet*'. Another tradition gave him Adam in *As You Like It*.[1] His name appears in the lists of Principal Comedians or Tragedians prefixed to plays by Ben Jonson, acted in 1598, 1599, and 1603, but not in any of six similar lists from 1605 to 1611 or later.[2] That rather suggests that he dropped acting in or about 1604. But he was still in some sense a 'fellow' of the King's men on 4 May 1605, and held financial interests in their theatres until at least 1612.[3] John Ward, who came to Stratford-on-Avon as vicar in 1662, records that Shakespeare in his elder days lived in the town and—presumably from there—supplied the stage with two plays every year.[4] The actual date of his retirement must remain uncertain. He had bought New Place in 1597, but apparently his cousin Thomas Greene was living there in 1609 and expected another year's occupation.[5]

Hamlet has shown us that Shakespeare took an interest, perhaps even a distracting interest, in the problems of acting, but as a critic more obviously than as a participant. There is sporadic criticism, direct or implied, elsewhere. In *Troilus and Cressida*, perhaps the next play after *Hamlet*, Patroclus, for the amusement of Achilles, 'pageants' the 'topless deputation' of Agamemnon. He behaves

---

[1] *William Shakespeare*, II. 188–9, 214, 253, 262, 265, 278, 289.
[2] Ibid., II. 71–5.   [3] Ibid., II. 67, 73.   [4] Ibid., II. 249.
[5] Ibid., II. 95–6.

> Like a strutting player, whose conceit
> Lies in his hamstring, and doth think it rich
> To hear the wooden dialogue and sound
> 'Twixt his stretch'd footing and the scaffoldage.
>
> (I. iii. 153–6.)

Criticism even breaks into the splendour of Cleopatra's end. She will not be taken back to Rome, which becomes London, for there

> The quick comedians
> Extemporally will stage us, and present
> Our Alexandrian revels; Antony
> Shall be brought drunken forth, and I shall see
> Some squeaking Cleopatra boy my greatness.   (V. ii. 216.)

Shakespeare and his audiences had suffered from that 'squeaking Cleopatra'. The criticism is not all contemptuous. In *Richard II*,

> As in a theatre, the eyes of men,
> After a well-grac'd actor leaves the stage,
> Are idly bent on him that enters next,
> Thinking his prattle to be tedious.   (V. ii. 23.)

And it is again the Globe itself, not Rome, which Shakespeare has in mind when Cassius says in *Julius Caesar*,

> How many ages hence
> Shall this our lofty scene be acted over
> In states unborn and accents yet unknown!   (III. i. 111.)

In *A Midsummer-Night's Dream* (I. ii; III. i; IV. i) the make-shifts and petty jealousies of the tiring-house become the mark for the arrows of Shakespeare's satire. It is a commonplace of criticism that his Richard III is essentially an actor, who can afford to listen ironically to the vaunt of his gull Buckingham, when he claims,

> Tut, I can counterfeit the deep tragedian;
> Speak and look back, and pry on every side,
> Tremble and start at wagging of a straw,
> Intending deep suspicion. Ghastly looks
> Are at my service, like enforced smiles;
> And both are ready in their offices,
> At any time, to grace my stratagems.   (III. v. 5.)

In *Henry V* Shakespeare approaches stage problems from another angle, accompanying the acted scenes with the running comment of the prologue and choruses, which are in substance

an elaborate apology for the incapacity of a theatrical representation to deal adequately with an heroic theme.

> But pardon, gentles all,
> The flat unraised spirits that hath dar'd
> On this unworthy scaffold to bring forth
> So great an object. Can this cockpit hold
> The vasty fields of France? Or may we cram
> Within this wooden O the very casques
> That did affright the air at Agincourt? (Prol. 8.)

The audience are bidden to

> Piece out our imperfections with your thoughts. (Ibid., 23.)

The players are dealing with things,

> Which cannot in their huge and proper life
> Be here presented. (v., Chorus, 5.)

So far I have been mainly considering Shakespeare's direct
comments on the stage of his own day. But there is more in it.
What was the reaction on Shakespeare's own mind of all this
tinsel make-believe, in which he inevitably moved? Hamlet,
considering 'the purpose of playing', tells us that its 'end, both
at the first and now, was and is, to hold, as 'twere, the mirror
up to nature; to show virtue her own feature, scorn her own
image, and the very age and body of the time his form and
pressure' (III. ii. 23). But, as we read the plays, does it not
sometimes seem as if the mirror were reversed, and that, in
Shakespeare's imagination, nature, that is to say, life itself,
were holding it up to the stage?

Dr. Caroline Spurgeon in a recent book has dealt at great
length with Shakespeare's imagery. She dwells, in particular,
on the extent to which it is drawn from the features of life, as
it may well have been lived in such a country town as Stratford-
on-Avon in Warwickshire—from gardens and orchards, from
aspects of the weather, from the seasons, from the flight of
birds, from horses, deer, falcons, even from the snail; above all
from rivers, in calm and still more in flood, which Dr. Spurgeon
thinks inspired no less than fifty-nine images. The Avon, she
believes, was an enduring memory. The analysis is interesting,
and will not be irrelevant to a later phase of my argument. But of
theatrical images, Dr. Spurgeon makes little. There are a small
number, she says, and notes two in *Romeo and Juliet* and three
in *Hamlet*.[1] But surely the plays are pervaded by theatrical

[1] *Shakespeare's Imagery* (1935), 45, 367, 370.

imagery. Life itself is presented in terms of a drama. We have all, I suppose, been brought up on the famous passage in *As You Like It* (II. vii. 136–66). The banished Duke begins it:

> Thou seest we are not all alone unhappy.
> This wide and universal theatre
> Presents more woeful pageants than the scene
> Wherein we play in.

The melancholy Jaques takes up the theme:

> All the world's a stage,
> And all the men and women merely players.
> They have their exits and their entrances,
> And one man in his time plays many parts,
> His acts being seven ages.

And he elaborates it for twenty-three lines more. It is not particularly appropriate to the action of the play itself, in which both the Duke and Jaques are spectators rather than participants. But it is a window into Shakespeare's mind, when he wrote it, not long before *Hamlet*. And even in this explicit form it has several echoes elsewhere. The melancholy Antonio in *The Merchant of Venice* says,

> I hold the world but as the world, Gratiano;
> A stage where every man must play his part,
> And mine a sad one.   (I. i. 77.)

Macbeth, faced with his ruin, comments,

> Life's but a walking shadow, a poor player
> That struts and frets his hour upon the stage
> And then is heard no more.   (V. v. 24.)

We recall the 'strutting player' of *Troilus and Cressida*. Lear, in his madness, declares,

> When we are born, we cry that we are come
> To this great stage of fools.   (IV. vi. 186.)

These are direct appreciations of life. But the same imagery is to be found, leaping almost unconsciously from Shakespeare's lips, in play after play, especially in those that deal with the changing fortunes of kings and heroes. In *2 Henry VI* Richard says of the enemies who plot his death,

> But mine is made the prologue to their play;
> For thousands more, that yet suspect no peril,
> Will not conclude their plotted tragedy.   (III. i. 151.)

In *3 Henry VI* Warwick comments on a battle,

> Why stand we like soft-hearted women here,
> Wailing our losses, whiles the foe doth rage;
> And look upon, as if the tragedy
> Were played in jest by counterfeiting actors?   (II. iii. 25.)

And at the end Henry, submitting to Richard, asks,

> What scene of death hath Roscius now to act?   (v. vi. 10.)

In *Richard III* the Duchess asks the distraught Elizabeth,

> What means this scene of rude impatience?

And she replies,

> To make an act of tragic violence.   (II. ii. 38.)

Later she is described as

> A queen in jest, only to fill the scene.   (IV. iv. 91.)

Richard the Second moralizes on 'the antic' Death, who sits within the hollow crown of a king,

> Allowing him a breath, a little scene,
> To monarchize, be feared, and kill with looks.   (III. ii. 164.)

And after his fall he summarizes his own meditations:

> Thus play I in one person many people,
> And none contented. Sometimes I am king;
> Then treasons make me wish myself a beggar,
> And so I am.   (v. v. 31.)

In *King John* the Bastard points to the 'scroyles of Angiers', who flout the kings,

> And stand securely on their battlements
> As in a theatre, whence they gape and point
> At your industrious scenes and acts of death.   (II. i. 374.)

In *2 Henry IV* Northumberland cries,

> Let order die!
> And let this world no longer be a stage
> To feed contention in a ling'ring act;
> But let one spirit of the first-born Cain
> Reign in all bosoms, that, each heart being set
> On bloody courses, the rude scene may end,
> And darkness be the burier of the dead.   (I. i. 154.)

Henry, on his death-bed, recalls his struggles to keep his kingdom in peace:

> For all my reign hath been but as a scene
> Acting that argument.   (IV. v. 198.)

In *Henry V* the Archbishop of Canterbury recalls the memory of the Black Prince,

> Who on the French ground play'd a tragedy.   (I. ii. 106.)

So, too, it is in the tragedies. In *Titus Andronicus*, after the murder of Bassianus, Tamora shows a fatal writ,

> The complot of this timeless tragedy.   (II. iii. 265.)

The same language runs through *Hamlet* itself, quite apart from the direct comments on acting. At the beginning signs in heaven and earth are 'prologue to the omen coming on' (I. i. 123). Hamlet's dress and behaviour are 'actions that a man might play' (I. ii. 84). Claudius is 'a vice of Kings' (III. iv. 98). In her trepidation after the death of Polonius, the Queen says,

> Each toy seems prologue to some great amiss.   (IV. v. 18.)

Hamlet describes his narrow escape from death at sea:

> Ere I could make a prologue to my brains,
> They had begun the play.   (V. ii. 30.)

Almost his last words are addressed to those,

> That are but mutes or audience to this act.   (V. ii. 346.)

Macbeth, learning the partial fulfilment of the witches' prophecy, through the death of Glamis and the fall of Cawdor, says,

> Two truths are told,
> As happy prologues to the swelling act
> Of the imperial theme.   (I. iii. 127.)

In the dark morning after the murder of Duncan, a bystander comments,

> Thou seest the heavens, as troubled with man's act,
> Threatens his bloody stage.   (II. iv. 5.)

In *Othello* the dead bodies of the Moor and Desdemona are 'the tragic loading of this bed' (V. ii. 363). Of Coriolanus, fighting as a youth with Tarquin, it is said,

> When he might act the woman in the scene,
> He proved best man i' the field.   (II. ii. 100.)

After his submission to his mother, he reflects,

> Behold the heavens do ope,
> The gods look down, and this unnatural scene
> They laugh at.   (V. iii. 183.)

Similar language is in the comedies and romances too, if

more rarely. Rosalind, in *As You Like It*, intervening in the
love affairs of Phoebe and Silvius, says,

> I'll prove a busy actor in their play.   (III. iv. 62.)

The Duke in *Measure for Measure*, declares,

> I love the people,
> But do not like to stage me to their eyes.   (I. i. 68.)

Cymbeline appeals to Imogen:

> How now, my flesh, my child!
> What, mak'st thou me a dullard in this act?
> Wilt thou not speak to me?   (v. v. 264.)

In *The Winter's Tale* Hermione declares that her past life

> Hath been as continent, as chaste, as true,
> As I am now unhappy, which is more
> Than history can pattern, though devis'd
> And play'd to take spectators.   (III. ii. 35.)

And of the recovery of Perdita it is said,

> The dignity of this act was worth the audience of kings and princes;
> for by such was it acted.   (v. ii. 86–8.)

These are all examples, by no means exhaustive, of definite
theatrical imagery. But even where that is not present, stage
terms seem in a subtle way to have affected Shakespeare's diction. What his characters have to say and do is their 'part'.
They are 'prompted' to speak or intervene. No doubt the
general senses of both words are historically prior to their
technical ones. A 'part' is a 'share'. To 'prompt' is to 'suggest'. But that Shakespeare uses them, as a man of the theatre
would use them, is often probable and sometimes certain.
Coriolanus says,

> Like a dull actor now,
> I have forgot my part, and I am out.   (v. iii. 40.)

Or he says,

> You have put me now to such a part which never
> I shall discharge to the life.

And Cominius answers,

> Come, come, we'll prompt you.   (III. ii. 105.)

Othello says,

> Were it my cue to fight, I should have known it
> Without a prompter.   (I. ii. 83.)

'Cue', a purely technical stage term for 'signal', occurs a dozen times in the plays. Particularly interesting is the constant use of the verb 'play' to indicate 'behave like'. This, indeed, did not begin with Shakespeare. Chaucer speaks of 'playing tyrant'. We have preserved the sense in a few cases. We play truant, or the man, or the knave, or the rogue, or the fool, or the devil, or 'old Harry', which is not Shakespearean, but first emerges in the eighteenth century. But Shakespeare's characters also play the dog, the cur, the spaniel, the sheep, the spider, the servant, the porter, the cook, the scribe, the good husband, the woman, the noble housewife, the Amazon, the wanton, the strumpet, the villain, the ruffian, the thief, the cheater, the traitor, the eaves-dropper, the saucy cuttle (whatever that may be), the runaway, the flouting Jack, the honest Trojan, the alchemist, the orator, the judge, the pious innocent, the penitent, the executioner, the recanter, the host, the umpire, the God. There is no end to it.

That Shakespeare's mind was permeated by the atmosphere of the stage, in which he lived and moved and had his being, seems to me indisputable. But did he realize it, and, if so, how did he react to it? There we are inevitably much in the dark. Did he come to feel some discontent with the limits imposed by theatrical conditions upon the creative imagination? Can we so explain the puzzling problem of the extreme and apparently unactable length of many of his plays, if no loophole can be found in the evidence as to the time available for performance? Did he write them for himself, and remain content to let the actors mangle them as they would? He never published them, but did he ever dream of publishing them? Tradition does not help us here. The reporters were interested in the playwright and what he has left us, not in his private ambitions and regrets. We turn to the sonnets, but that is largely interpreting the obscure by the obscurer still. Did he take refuge from the artificial life, to which he seemed bound, in the casual amours of which some of them seem to tell, or in that friendship which apparently failed him in the end? The record, if it is a record, is too blurred to be legible now. The earlier sonnets have occasionally something of the stage imagery in them, although not very much.

> When I consider every thing that grows
> Holds in perfection but a little moment,
> That this huge stage presenteth nought but shows
> Whereon the stars in secret influence comment. (xv.)

And again:

> As an unperfect actor on the stage,
> Who with his fear is put besides his part,
> Or some fierce thing replete with too much rage,
> Whose strength's abundance weakens his own heart,
> So I, for fear of trust, forget to say
> The perfect ceremony of love's rite.   (XXIII.)

And they are largely concerned with something Shakespeare does not readily accept in his own life.

> Let those, who are in favour with their stars,
> Of public honour and proud titles boast,
> Whilst I, whom Fortune of such triumph bars,
> Unlook'd for joy in that I honour most.   (XXV.)

He is 'in disgrace with Fortune and men's eyes' (XXIX) and thinks himself in some way under a cloud.

> I may not ever more acknowledge thee,
> Lest my bewailed guilt should do thee shame.   (XXXVI.)

He has been 'made lame by Fortune's dearest spite', but, through living by a part of his friend's glory, is no longer 'lame, poor, nor despised' (XXXVII). The same image recurs in another sonnet.

> Speak of my lameness, and I straight will halt.   (LXXXIX.)

Many inept things have been written about the *Sonnets*, but I think that the prize for ineptitude must go to the gentleman who inferred from these passages that Shakespeare was lame.

A similar note is traceable in some of the later sonnets, written three or more years after the first meeting with the friend. The poet has made himself 'a motley to the view', which rather suggests the stage fool, and 'vulgar scandal' has stamped an impression on his brow. But the most significant sonnet is surely CXI, which begins:

> O for my sake do you with Fortune chide,
> The guilty goddess of my harmful deeds,
> That did not better for my life provide
> Than public means which public manners breeds.
> Thence comes it that my name receives a brand,
> And almost thence my nature is subdued
> To what it works in, like the dyer's hand.

Can the brand be anything else than an allusion to the status of an actor, about which, in Elizabethan eyes, the old tradition of the infamous *histrio* of the early Fathers still clung? And the

dyer's hand, stained with his dyes—does not that reflect a consciousness in Shakespeare himself that his imagination was so
hopelessly imbued with the colour given to it by his profession,
that he could only see things as they were reflected in the mirror
of the stage?

> I cannot look on life
> Alone and plainly.

They are not his own words, but they will serve. This sonnet
comes later in the series than that (CVII) on the eclipse of the
mortal moon, which has been much discussed, but which I
believe to have been written in 1599 or early in 1600, shortly
after the fear of a Spanish invasion, which led to rumours that
Queen Elizabeth was dead. 'Mortua sed non sepulta', said
the indomitable old lady. This other may therefore date from
just about the time when Shakespeare was writing *Hamlet*,
which shows his preoccupation with the stage at its height, to
an extent which perhaps rather embarrasses the movement of
the play. And after *Hamlet* came a group of plays which, to
some readers at least, show Shakespeare in a rather uncomfort-
able mood: the bitter comedies of *Alls' Well* and *Measure for
Measure*, and *Troilus and Cressida*, the comedy, if you will, but
rather, as I think, the tragedy, of disillusionment with the world's
ancient ideals of heroism and romance.

And, a little later, we find Shakespeare ceasing to appear as
a Principal Tragedian or Comedian in play-prints. Was he
glad to be no longer one of those whom a Dame Quickly could
call 'harlotry players'?[1] Was he hoping to purify his imagination from its taint? Ultimately—we do not know quite when
—he retired to Stratford. Here, among the young mulberries
he had planted, he could write his plays, send them, as Parson
Ward tells us, to the stage at the rate of two a year, and never
trouble about what happened to them afterwards. Most of the
longest plays are later than *Hamlet*. They include *Troilus and
Cressida*, *Othello*, *Lear*, *Antony and Cleopatra*, *Coriolanus*, and
Cymbeline. But several of the histories, which came earlier, are
also long. The later tragedies are more as Aristotle would have
them, more concerned with the emotions evoked by the fundamental issues of life and less with the interpretation of character
in action, than *Hamlet*. If Shakespeare ever dreamt of printing his *Works*, like Ben Jonson, it came to nothing. He never
quite purged his bosom of the perilous stuff that had troubled

---

[1] *1 Hen. IV*, II. iv. 437.

him. The stage imagery is still traceable in the later plays, although not, I think, quite so frequent. But at least he could sweeten his imagination again with the scents and sounds of rural life, watching the movements of the clouds and the changing moods of his native Avon. Dr. Spurgeon aptly notes his preoccupation in *Cymbeline* with 'the background of trees, the fragrance of flowers and the presence of birds', and in particular the culmination of the play in the reconciliation of Posthumus and Imogen, when he murmurs,

> Hang there like fruit, my soul,
> Till the tree die. (v. v. 263.)

Stratford was real. Here a tired poet might rest his eyes in Perdita's garden, gathering, if not the daffodils and violets dim of youth, at least such flowers of middle summer, as are given to men of middle age:

> Hot lavender, mints, savory, marjoram;
> The marigold, that goes to bed wi' the sun
> And with him rises weeping. (*W.T.* iv. iv. 104.)

And returning to New Place, Shakespeare sent John Fletcher a scrap to be put into *The Two Noble Kinsmen*:

> O Queen Emilia,
> Fresher than May, sweeter
> Than her gold buttons on the boughs, or all
> Th' enamelled knacks o' th' mead or garden, yea,
> We challenge too the bank of any nymph,
> That makes the stream seem flowers. (iii. i. 4.)

With these lovely lines of the recovered sanity of life I will end my speculation.

1940.

WILLIAM SHAKESHAFTE

In my *Elizabethan Stage* of 1923 (i. 280) I quoted a passage
from a will executed on 3 August 1581 by Alexander Houghton
of Lea, Lancashire, in which, after making a legacy of his stock
of play clothes to his brother Thomas, or if he should not wish
to keep players, then to Sir Thomas Heskethe, he added a
request to Sir Thomas to be friendly to Foke Gyllome and
William Shakshafte, then dwelling with the testator, and either
to take them into his service or else to help them to a good
master. And I added the comment, 'Was then William Shakshafte a player in 1581?' The will was proved on 12 September 1581, and a text of it was printed by G. J. Piccope in the
second part of his *Lancashire and Cheshire Wills* (1860,
Chetham Soc., li. 237). More recently it has been discussed
by the late Oliver Baker (1937, *In Shakespeare's Warwickshire
and the Unknown Years*, 297 sqq.), who gave a photographic
facsimile of part of the original, preserved in the Ecclesiastical
Court at Chester. Unfortunately it is a very bad one, since it
has been so taken as to cut off the opening words of each line.
With its help, however, it is possible to make some minor
corrections in Piccope's version, which is not quite accurate,
and in part a summary, rather than a literal transcript. The
following is as near as I can get in war-time to a correct version
of the most important passage. Abbreviations in the facsimile
are italicized. Brynescoules may be Brinscall, Lancashire.

Item yt ys my mynd *and* wyll that Thomas Houghton of Brynescoules
my brother shall haue all my Instrument*es* belonginge to mewsyckes *and*
all man*er* of playe clothes yf he be mynded to keppe *and* doe keppe
playeres. And yf he wyll not keppe and manteyne playeres then yt ys my
wyll that *Sir* Thomas Heskethe knyghte shall haue the same Instrument*es*
and playe clothes. And I most hertelye requyre the said *Sir* Thomas to be
ffrendlye unto ffoke Gyllome and Will*iam* Shakeshafte nowe dwellynge
with me *and* eyther to take theym vnto his Servyce or els to helpe theym
to some good *master* as my tryste ys he wyll.

The linking with Sir Thomas Heskethe seems to make it at least
highly probable that Foke Gyllome and William Shakeshafte
were players. The will goes on, firstly to provide for the payment of a year's wages to every servant of the testator at the
time of his death, and secondly to recite a provision in an entail, dated on 20 July 1580, of his landed property upon his

brother Thomas, which reserved an annual rent-charge of £16. 13*s*. 4*d*. to be spent in the provision of annuities for some of these servants, who are now named. There are eleven of them. One gets £3. 6*s*. 8*d*., four £1, two 13*s*. 4*d*., and four £2. Among these last are William Shakeshafte and Fowke Gyllom, and also a Thomas Gyllome. There is a further direction that, on the death of any annuitant, his share is to be divided among those still living, so that the last survivor shall get for his life the whole amount of the rent-charge. A generous, if meticulous old gentleman! His wife Elizabeth is to be executrix, or, failing her, his brother-in-law Thomas Heskethe, of Gray's Inn, executor. His brother-in-law, Bartholomew Heskethe, is to be a supervisor. He is also a witness to the will.

I do not know why I did not refer again in my *William Shakespeare* (1930) to this William Shakeshafte, which, rather than Shakshafte, is the normal spelling of the will, although I noted the numerous variations in the spelling of the name Shakespeare, the not infrequent appearance of Shakeshaft, an example of a Shakeschaft and a Shakestaff holding land together in Shropshire, and in particular the fact that the poet's grandfather, Richard, seems to be both Shakstaff and Shakeschafte, as well as Shakspere, Shakespere, Shakkespere, and Shaxpere, in the Snitterfield manor records (*W.S.*, ii. 27, 372). I do not think that his father John ever appears as Shakeshafte, but it is at least conceivable that William might have adopted the variant as a player. It does not, of course, recur in his London career. Baker notes the existence of a Gillom family at Bidford and at Henley-in-Arden, where ancestors of my own once lived—both in the neighbourhood of Stratford; and also the fact that the name Foke or Fulke was more common in Warwickshire than elsewhere in England. This is perhaps due to the three successive Fulke Grevilles of Beauchamp Court. The last of these, who became Lord Brooke, is said by David Lloyd in 1665 to have desired 'to be known to posterity under no other notions than of *Shakespear's* and *Ben Johnson's* Master, Chancellor *Egerton's* Patron, Bishop *Overal's* Lord, and Sir *Philip Sidney's* friend' (*W.S.*, ii. 250). No explanation of this allusion to Shakespeare has ever been found. Greville's official posts would not obviously bring him into contact with players. It is conceivable that a company may have been maintained at Beauchamp Court, but there is no evidence of it.

I now return, however, to the William Shakeshafte of 1581,

because I have come upon a good deal about the Houghton and Hesketh families, which escaped my observation in 1923. It is largely taken from the edition by F. R. Raines of *The Derby Household Books* (1853, Chetham Soc., xxxi). Here is a record of the weekly expenses of Henry Stanley, fourth Earl of Derby, at his houses of Knowsley, Lathom, and New Park in Lancashire, kept by his steward William Farington, and accompanied by notes of the coming and going of the Stanleys and their visitors during each week. Both Houghtons and Heskeths often make their appearance among these.

Alexander Houghton was of course dead before the record begins. But in June 1587 came Mr. Auditor Houghton, whom Raines takes to be Thomas Houghton of Houghton Towers. But he was also of Lea, which he had acquired under the entail of 1580. He came again, with his son Richard, then a lad of seventeen, in October, and again, apparently to join his wife Anne, in December, and yet again in January 1589. On 21 November 1589 he was slain in a fray at Lea with Thomas Langton, Baron Newton, of Walton Hall. Some details of this affair are given by Baker from historians of Lancashire. There is no mention of Brynescoules, but that of Lea clearly identifies this Thomas Houghton with the brother Thomas of Alexander's will. The Earl of Derby seems to have been much concerned about the event. The Baron, too, had often been one of his visitors. He rode to Preston, 'to see peace &c.', and in January 1590 there was a great company of lawyers at his house to discuss the affair, including Thomas Hesketh of Gray's Inn, Alexander Houghton's brother-in-law and executor. Visits were also paid during the winter and spring by his other brother-in-law, Bartholomew Hesketh. Meanwhile both Richard Houghton and the Baron came and went, and in the end, rightly or wrongly—for who shall say, when an Earl intervenes?—the Baron was acquitted of manslaughter at the Assizes. A last visit by Richard Houghton is recorded in June 1590, and thereafter the family drops out of Farington's story. From other sources I learn that Anne, the widow of Thomas Houghton, then still of Lea, was ordered to custody as a Catholic recusant in October 1592 (*Calendar Hatfield MSS.*, iv. 242; Baker, 303), and that in February 1594 a yellow-haired Hesketh, whose Christian name is not given, was alleged to have said at Prague that he left Lancashire for the slaughter of Mr. Houghton (*Cal. Hatf. MSS.*, iv. 481).

I turn now to Sir Thomas Hesketh and his family, and their connexion with the Stanleys. Sir Thomas was of Rufford, Lancashire. Thomas Hesketh of Gray's Inn, Bartholomew, his brother, and Elizabeth Houghton, his sister, were relations, but came from a different branch of the family, being children of Gabriel Hesketh of Aughton, Lancashire. Sir Thomas came to the Earl of Derby's house on 25 May 1587 and again on the following 30 December. Farington's note on this second occasion is rather an odd one, and I shall have to revert to it. It runs, 'On Saturday Sʳ Tho. Hesketh, Players went awaie'. Sir Thomas came again in January 1588, with a son. Baker says that he died in 1587. But that is obviously an error. Raines gives an abstract of his will, which is dated on 20 June 1588. He left three legitimate sons by his wife, Alice Holcroft, Robert, who was his heir, Thomas, and Richard. An executor was again Thomas Hesketh of Gray's Inn. I think there can be no doubt that the *D.N.B.* is wrong in identifying this son Richard with the Richard Hesketh, a Catholic intriguer, who was executed in 1593, for attempting to persuade Ferdinando, Earl of Derby, to put forward a claim to the crown of England in succession to Elizabeth. There are several documents about this affair among the Hatfield archives, and it is clear from them that he was a brother of Bartholomew, who was himself regarded in 1592 as a dangerous person, if not actually a recusant. Thomas of Gray's Inn, on the other hnad, although he thought that the Earl of Derby had dealt hardly with his brother, seems to have been a loyalist (*Cal. Hatf. MSS.*, iv. 127, 241, 381, 389, 390, 402, 407, 408, 409, 411, 418, 421, 423, 425, 427, 428, 461; v. 58, 277, 360, 369, 390; xiii. 493). The will of Sir Thomas Hesketh contains no clear evidence that he maintained players. There are annuities for two servants, Degory Rishton and John Spenser. It may be coincidence that the manuscript of the *Parnassus* plays was owned about 1605 by one 'Edmunde Rishton, Lancastrensis', and that a John Spencer was an English actor in Germany during 1605–23 (*Elizabethan Stage*, ii. 341; iv. 38). After the date of Sir Thomas Hesketh's will, Lady Hesketh was at Lord Derby's house in October 1588, with a son, presumably Robert, the heir, who was also there in June 1589 and in February and May 1590.

The Stanleys maintained players through many years. Earl Henry had a company from an early date, but it is not heard of after 1582. Probably it passed to his son Ferdinando, Lord Strange, who himself became Earl in 1593. I need not go again into the complicated history of his players, who are first recorded in 1576–7, when he was little more than a boy, are sometimes described as tumblers or performers of activities, and stood at various times in relations with one John Symons, and with other groups under the patronage of the Lord Admiral Howard, the Earls of Oxford and Pembroke, and the Queen herself, up to Earl Ferdinando's death in 1594, when a final shuffle left the domination of the London stage to Lord Hunsdon's company at the Theatre and the Lord Admiral's at the Rose (*E.S.*, ii. 118–27; *W.S.*, i. 27–56). Lord Strange was often at his father's Lancashire houses, and there are many records of visits by players—the Earl of Leicester's in July 1587, the Queen's in October 1588, July and September 1589, and June 1590, and the Earl of Essex's in September 1589. Of others, in December 1588, January 1589, and February 1590, the patrons are not named. On the first of these occasions Farington notes, 'a Playe was had in the Halle, & the same nyght my L. Strandge came home'; on the second only 'the Plaiers plaied'; on the third 'Players played at nyght'. I think it possible that these anonymous players were Strange's own men. Certainly he seems to have been at his father's house on all the three days concerned. I have already noted the rather ambiguous entry for 30 December 1587, 'Sᵗ Tho. Hesketh, Players went awaie'. Farington had not previously noted the coming of either of them. His jottings are sometimes rough, but I should like to be sure about that comma.[1] Could he have written 'Hesketh *and*' or 'Hesketh*es*'? That, however, is the sort of point, which it is impossible to pursue in war-time. In any case it is clear that, if William Shakeshafte passed from the service of Alexander Houghton into that of either Thomas Houghton or Sir Thomas Hesketh, he might very easily have gone on into that of Lord Strange, and so later into the London theatrical world, where we find in 1592 William Shakespeare, writing probably for Lord Pembroke's men, and called by the envious Robert Greene 'the only Shake-scene in a countrey' (*W.S.*, i. 287; ii. 188).

1943.

[1] I now (12 Oct. 1944) learn that the comma is an editorial addition by Raines to Farington's MS. which has none.

THE thanks of *The Library* are due to the Marquis of Bath for his courteous permission to reproduce the attached drawing and script by Henry Peacham, artist, schoolmaster, epigrammatist, and pamphleteer, from vol. i, f. 159^v, of the *Harley Papers* at Longleat.[1] Whatever may be thought of the relation of Peacham's text to *Titus Andronicus*, the drawing is at least of interest as the first known illustration to any play of the Shakespearean canon. Incidentally it may inform students of *Othello*, as well as of *Titus*, that to the Elizabethan mind a Moor was not tawny but dead black. ·

The document was calendared by Mrs. S. C. Lomas in 1907 (*H. M. Comm., Longleat Papers*, ii. 43), but has not received much, if any, attention from writers on Shakespeare. It consists of a single sheet, endorsed on a spare page—

This perhaps enables us to interpret the rather cryptic date 'Anno m° q° q q^{to}', which Peacham has written against the script, beneath his own name, although the 'q^{to}' taken by itself might represent either 'quinto' or 'quarto', and, unless 'q' is a slip for an arabic 9, it is difficult to see how it can represent 'nono'. Most of the Elizabethan papers in the composite volume were brought from Welbeck to Longleat by Lady Elizabeth Bentinck in 1759, and derive ultimately from the study of Sir Michael Hicks, a secretary to the first Lord Burghley. This may be one of them, although Mrs. Lomas does not identify the hand of the endorsement, which is not that of either Burghley or Hicks, and a pencilled reference in the margin to the second Sir John Thynne (1580–1623) may suggest that it had been preserved since the sixteenth century at Longleat itself. No doubt Peacham, born at North Mimms, is more likely *a priori* to have been in touch with Theobalds than with Longleat.

[1] The drawing is now again reproduced as a frontispiece to this volume.

I now give the text of the script which accompanies the
drawing, and a collation of its variants, other than those of
mere orthography, which are numerous, from the correspond
ing passages of Q_2 (1600) and F_1 (1623) of *Titus Andronicus*
Obviously, if Peacham used any extant print, it would be Q
(1594). The only known copy is in the collection of Mr. H. C
Folger, and has not, I believe, been reproduced. The collation
by E. Ljunggren in *Shakespeare-Jahrbuch*, xli. 211, shows no
divergences as regards these passages from Q_2, except 'hay
stalkes' for 'haystakes' in l. 31, where the 'haystackes' of
the manuscript agrees with F_1. But Ljunggren also neglects
mere orthographic variants, and it is possible that the
manuscript might prove to be generally closer as regards
spelling to Q_1 than to Q_2. Punctuation the manuscript has
none.

Enter Tamora pleadinge for her sonnes going to
execution

Tam: Stay Romane bretheren gratious Conquerors
Victorious Titus rue the teares I shed
A mothers teares in passion of her sonnes
And if thy sonnes were ever deare to thee
Oh thinke my sonnes to bee as deare to mee
Suffizeth not that wee are brought to Roome
To beautify thy triumphes and returne
Captiue to thee and to thy Romane yoake   10
But must my sonnes be slaughtered in the streetes
for valiant doinges in there Cuntryes cause
Oh if to fight for kinge and Common weale
Were piety in thine it is in these
Andronicus staine not thy tombe *with* blood   1
Wilt thou drawe neere the nature of the God*es*
Drawe neere them then in being mercifull
Sweete mercy is nobilityes true badge
Thrice noble Titus spare my first borne sonne

Titus: Patient your selfe madame for dy hee must   2
Aaron do you likewise prepare your selfe
And now at last repent your wicked life

1–2 Enter . . . execution] Q_2 (1. i. 70) . . . enter . . . Tamora the Queene of
Gothes and her two sonnes, Chiron and Demetrius, with Aron (F_1 Aaron) the
More . . .   3–20 Tam: Stay . . . madame = 1. i. 104–21 *as in* Q_2 F_1, *which
end the last line with* and pardon me.   3 Conquerors] Q_2 Conquerer; F_1
Conqueror.   5 of her sonnes] Q_2 F_1 for her sonne.   7 sonnes] Q_2 sonne;
F_1 sonnes.   20–2 for . . . life] Q_2 F_1 *omit*.

Aron: Ah now I curse the day and yet I thinke
few comes within the compasse of my curse
Wherein I did not some notorious ill 25
As kill a man or els devise his death
Ravish a mayd or plott the way to do it
Acuse some innocent and forsweare my selfe
Set deadly enmity betweene too freend*es*
Make poore mens cattell breake theire neckes 30
Set fire on barnes and haystackes in the night
And bid the owners quench them *with* their teares
Oft have I digd vp dead men from their graves
And set them vpright at their deere frend*es* dore
Even almost when theire sorrowes was forgott 35
And on their brestes as on the barke of trees
Have with my knife carvd in Romane letters
Lett not your sorrowe dy though I am dead
Tut I have done a thousand dreadfull thinges
As willingly as one would kill a fly 40
And nothing greives mee hartily indeede
for that I cannot doo ten thousand more & *cetera*
  Alarbus

23–42 Aron: Ah ... more = v. i. 125–44 *as in* $Q_2 F_1$, *which have no* '&
etera'. 23 Ah] $Q_2 F_1$ Euen 24 comes] $Q_2 F_1$ come. the] F_1 few. 31 hay-
stackes] Q_1 haystalkes; Q_2 haystakes; F_1 Haystackes. 32 their teares] F_1 the
teares. 35 Even almost when theire sorrowes] $Q_2 F_1$ Euen when their sorrowes
almost. 36 brestes] $Q_2 F_1$ skinnes. 37 carvd] $Q_2 F_1$ carued. 42 for]
$Q_2 F_1$ But. 43 Alarbus] *This character has no speech in* $Q_2 F_1$.

It will be seen that the speeches of Tamora and Aaron in
the manuscript, but for the omission of the first line of Aaron's
(v. i. 124), are substantially identical with those in the prints;
and the slight verbal variants, even that of 'brestes' for 'skinnes',
are not in themselves beyond the compass of a transcriber more
intent upon his penmanship than his textual accuracy. But
there are some odd features to be recorded. In the first place,
while the references to Tamora's sons are not absolutely consistent either in the prints or in the manuscript, it is clear that
the death of one only, Alarbus, is contemplated in the former,
and equally clear that the death of at least two is contemplated
in the latter. And this is confirmed by the drawing, which
shows two bound captives kneeling behind Tamora. Secondly,
in the prints Alarbus never speaks, but the manuscript ends
with a speech-prefix for him. And thirdly, in the prints Aaron,
although present, does not speak in the supplication scene, but

in the manuscript he is given a speech which the prints put in v. i, and this is linked to Tamora's by two lines and a half for Titus, which are not in the prints at all. This is not necessitated by the drawing, in which the posture of Aaron—for the black figure must be Aaron and not an executioner—would need no alteration, if he were merely championing the princes and were not on his own defence at all. Are we then to infer that Peacham had before him an early version of the play and that this was afterwards rearranged? It would be a hazardous conclusion, and it would of course be more hazardous still to suggest that Peacham was the 'private author' whose work, according to the tradition reported by Edward Ravenscroft in 1687, was touched up by Shakespeare. Peacham only took his bachelor's degree in 1595, the year of the sketch, and *Titus Andronicus* seems to have been played in some form by Sussex's men in January 1594, if not also by Strange's men in April 1592. And although Peacham saw Tarlton as a boy, and has allusions to the life of the theatre here and there in his epigrams and pamphlets, there is no indication outside the manuscript that he was ever a playwright. But why he should have perverted the Quarto text for the purpose of making an illustration of it, it is difficult to see.

A friend suggests to me that the sheet may have been done by Peacham for a competition in penmanship, and cites as an analogy the sets of verses on *Ecclesiasticus*, of which one is reproduced by Mr. McKerrow in his edition of Nashe (iii. 298). He may be right, although I do not see anything, in either case, which points very clearly to a competition. But a reason for the manipulation of the text would still be to seek. In general design the sheet is not unlike the pages of woodcut emblems in Peacham's *Minerva Britanna* (1612) or the coloured illustrations to King James's *Basilicon Doron* in Royal MS. 12 A, lxvi, which he gave to Prince Henry in 1610.

1925.

THE OCCASION OF *A MIDSUMMER-NIGHT'S DREAM*

IT has long been recognized that the epithalamic ending of *A Midsummer-Night's Dream* points to performance at a wedding, and that the compliment to the 'fair vestal throned by the west' points to a wedding at which Queen Elizabeth was present. The most plausible date hitherto suggested is 26 January 1595, on which William Stanley, Earl of Derby, married the Lady Elizabeth Vere, daughter of the Earl of Oxford, granddaughter of William, Lord Burghley, and goddaughter and maid of honour to the Queen. This would fit in well enough with the allusions in the play to the bad weather of 1594, and to the lion at the baptism of Prince Henry of Scotland on 30 August of the same year; while the presence of Elizabeth has been inferred from the words of Stowe, who says that 'The 26 of January William Earl of Derby married the Earl of Oxford's daughter at the court then at Greenwich, which marriage feast was there most royally kept'. I have long been puzzled by the statement that the wedding was 'at the court'; not so much because the Treasurer of the Chamber made no payment for a court play on 26 January 1595, since the performance might have been ordered, not by the Queen, but by the friends of the bride or bridegroom, as because the wedding itself does not appear in the list of those solemnized in the royal chapel and closet which is preserved in the so-called 'Cheque-Book' of the Chapel (ed. E. F. Rimbault, 160), and I have now good reason to think that Stowe made a mistake on this point, for in the accounts of the churchwardens of St. Martin's, Westminster (ed. J. V. Kitto, 471), I find for the year 1595 the following entry:

> Item paid the xxx[th] of January for ringinge At her Ma[ties] Comynge to y[e] Lord Threasurers to y[e] Earle of Darbies weddinge And at her Departure from thence y[e] fyrst of ffebruary ij[s].

The court appears, indeed, to have been established at Greenwich from the middle of December 1594 to the middle of February 1595. But it was not uncommon for Elizabeth, especially in her somewhat restless old age, to leave the court for a day or two's sojourn with some favoured courtier in

61

London or the neighbouring villages; and it was evidently upon
such an occasion that she did honour to the nuptials of Elizabeth Vere at Burghley House in the Strand. There is no entry
of the marriage in the registers of St. Martin's or of St.
Clement Danes, in which parishes Burghley House stood, and
I think it is probable that it took place in the chapel of the
Savoy, hard by, the registers of which are lost, for a contemporary record of another wedding, a few years later, tells us
(*H.M.C., Rutland MSS.* i. 379):

The feast was held here at Burghley howse. M^rs bryde with her hayre
hanging downe was led betwen two yong bachelors from Burghley
Howse thorough the streete, strawed, to the Savoy gate against my lodg-
ing, and so to that church.

I do not think that it is necessary, on the strength of the St.
Martin's entry, to reject Stowe's date as well as his locality.
The bell-ringings for Elizabeth's removals are often entered
with only approximate accuracy, possibly because the churchwardens recorded the dates of the payments rather than those
of the services rendered. And Stowe's 26 January can in fact
be confirmed from another source. On 27 January Anthony
Bacon wrote from London to Francis Bacon at Twickenham,
telling him that Antonio Perez had highly commended the
Queen's grace and the royal magnificence of some court
solemnity then on hand (T. Birch, *Elizabeth,* i. 199), and this
crossed a letter of the same date from Francis to Anthony
(Spedding, *Life and Letters,* i. 353), in which he said:

I hope by this time Antonio Perez hath seen the Queen dance (that is
not it, but her disposition of body to be fresh and good I pray God both
subjects and strangers may long be witnesses of). I would be sorry the
bride and bridegroom should be as the weather hath fallen out, that is go
to bed fair and rise lowring.

Spedding could not identify the bride and bridegroom, but
there can be no doubt about them. Elizabeth, of course, was
ready to dance on the edge of her grave; Burghley, the master
of the feast, old and gouty, was for other than for dancing
measures. He had written to Robert Cecil on 2 December
(T. Wright, *Elizabeth and her Times,* ii. 440):

For her hope to have me dance, I must have a longer tyme to learn to
go, but I will be ready in mynd to dance with my hart, when I shall
behold her favorable disposition to do such honor to her mayd, for the
old man's sake.

And on 2 January he added:

Though my hand is unable to fight, and my right eye unable to take a levell, yet they both do stoop to return my humble thankes for continuance of her favor at this tyme, when I am more fitter for an hospital, than to be a party for a marriage.

These notices of the wedding indicate a mask, rather than a play; but the two would not be incompatible. The internal evidence of *A Midsummer-Night's Dream* does not take us much farther. The much-travelled Theseus might have been thought appropriate to William Stanley, whose own travels are said to have taken him as far as the Holy Land and Russia, and in later Lancashire legends grew to quite mythical proportions. There is the famous passage in which occurs the compliment to Elizabeth. The attempts of the older commentators to turn the mermaid and the falling stars and the little western flower into an allegory of Mary Queen of Scots and the northern rebellion, or of the intrigue of Leicester with the Countess of Essex, may be summarily disregarded. Whatever else complimentary poetry is, it must be in the first place gratifying to the person complimented, and in the second place reasonably topical. The northern rebellion and Leicester's marriage were both forgotten far-off things in 1595, nor was either of them calculated to give Elizabeth much pleasure in the retrospect. The marriage in particular had caused her bitter mortification in its day, and if Edmund Tilney had allowed Shakespeare to allude to it before her, he would have signed his own warrant for the Tower, and Shakespeare's for the Marshalsea. What Shakespeare was describing was, as it professed to be, a water-pageant with fireworks. But again, it is only a want of historical perspective or a sentimental desire to find a reminiscence of Shakespeare's childhood in his plays, which can explain the common identification of this water-pageant with that given at Kenilworth as far back as 1575. The princely pleasures of Kenilworth loom large to us out of the fragmentary records of Elizabeth's progresses, because they were set down in a racy pamphlet at the time, and because Scott used them as material for a novel. But there were many such entertainments both before and after, and if Shakespeare had any particular one in mind, it is far more likely to have been that which had occurred comparatively recently, when Elizabeth visited the Earl of Hertford at Elvetham in September 1591. As a matter of fact, there was not a mermaid on a dolphin's back either at Kenil-

worth or at Elvetham. At Kenilworth there was a Triton on a
mermaid's back, which is not quite the same thing. There was
the Lady of the Lake, who might perhaps be called a sea-maid.
And there was Arion on a dolphin's back, who sang to the
music of instruments in the dolphin's belly. There were fireworks also, but apparently not on the same day as the water-
pageant. At Elvetham there was 'a pompous aray of sea-
persons', including Nereus, five Tritons, Neptune, and
Oceanus, with 'other sea-gods' and a train in 'ouglie marine
suites'. They brought in Neaera, the 'sea-nymph', who sang
a ditty. Meanwhile a 'snail-mount' in the water resembled 'a
monster, having hornes of wild-fire continuously burning'; but
here also the principal display of fireworks was on another day.
Obviously, so far as subject-matter goes, Elvetham might, just
as well as Kenilworth, have furnished the motive for the extremely sketchy reminiscences of Oberon. It may be added
that at Elvetham the queen of the fairies, not for the first time
in the history of Elizabethan pageantry, had made her appearance. She is called Aureola, not Titania, but names the king
as Auberon. It goes without saying that Cupid all armed is
not mentioned in either account. He could only be seen by
Oberon. But it is to Cupid and the wound inflicted by his bolt
on the little western flower that the whole description leads up.
The flower has a part in the action of the play, and possibly
we ought not to seek for any further motive for its introduction. But if it points, as some think, to an enamoured woman,
how can this possibly be Lady Essex, or anybody else but the
bride in whose glorification, next only to that of Elizabeth, the
play was written? I do not assert that William Stanley and
Elizabeth Vere, then sixteen, met and loved at Elvetham in
1591. Indeed, as will be seen before the end of this article,
I do not assert that William Stanley and Elizabeth Vere were
the bridegroom and bride of the play at all. But Elizabeth
Vere, as one of the queen's maids, is at least likely to have been
there, and William Stanley, who was coming and going in
1589 and 1590 between London and his father's houses in the
north (*Stanley Papers*, ii. 66, 78, 82), may quite well have been
there too. Elizabeth Vere's marriage had been one of the pre-
occupations of Lord Burghley, who had evidently taken over
the responsibilities of her fantastic father, the Earl of Oxford,
for some years before 1595. Early in 1591, the Earl of Bedford was spoken of (*S. P. Dom. Eliz.* ccxxxviii. 69), but it came

to nothing, and Bedford married 'the Muses' evening, as their morning, star', Lucy Harington. About 1592 Burghley had been making suit for the Earl of Northumberland, 'but my Lady Veare hath answered her grandfather that she can not fancye him' (*H.M.C.*, *Rutland MSS.* i. 300). William Stanley was at this time only an undistinguished younger son, and Burghley, perhaps the greatest of our civil servants, had the civil servant's not uncommon foible for founding a dynasty. It was in 1594 that the deaths in rapid succession of his father and his elder brother left Stanley the most eligible match in England.

Philostrate offers as a wedding device the 'satire keen and critical', of—

> The thrice three Muses mourning for the death
> Of Learning, late deceased in beggary.

This has been regarded as support for the Stanley-Vere identification, on the ground that Spenser's *Tears of the Muses* was dedicated in 1591 to Lady Strange, the wife of Stanley's brother and predecessor in the title. I have used the argument myself, but I now doubt its validity. It is not at all clear that this lady would have been at the wedding. There was bitter feud in 1595 between her and her brother-in-law over the succession to the Derby estates, and already on 9 May 1594, she had written to Burghley (*H.M.C.*, *Hatfield MSS.* iv. 527):

> I hear of a motion of marriage between the Earl, my brother, and my Lady Vere, your niece, but how true the news is I know not, only I wish her a better husband.

One wonders how far Lady Derby was cognizant of the rumours sedulously spread about the country by the Jesuits as to the death of the late Earl, which had been sudden, had suggested suspicions of poisoning or witchcraft, and had robbed the Catholic intriguers of a hoped-for pretender. One version (*H.M.C.*, *Hatfield MSS.* v. 253) ascribed a crime to 'my lord that now is'; another (*S. P. Dom. Eliz.* ccxlix. 92) to Burghley, in order that he might marry the young Lady Vere to the Earl's brother. I now come to the rather curious fact that at the Stanley-Vere wedding there actually does appear to have been a show of the nine muses, although it was not in the least concerned with 'Learning, late deceased in beggary'. This emerges from a letter written by Arthur Throgmorton to Robert Cecil (*H.M.C.*, *Hatfield MSS.* v. 99). It is a curious side-light, not merely upon the methods, but upon some of the underlying motives of Elizabethan pageantry.

Matter of mirth from a good mind can minister no matter of malice, both being, as I believe, far from such sourness (and for myself I will answer for soundness). I am bold to write my determination, grounded upon grief and true duty to the Queen, thankfulness to my lord of Derby, (whose honourable brother honoured my marriage) and to assure you I bear no spleen to yourself. If I may I mind to come in a masque, brought in by the nine muses, whose music, I hope, shall so modify the easy softened mind of her Majesty as both I and mine may find mercy. The song, the substance I have herewith sent you, myself, whilst the singing, to lie prostrate at her Majesty's feet till she says she will save me. Upon my resurrection the song shall be delivered by one of the muses, with a ring made for a wedding ring set round with diamonds, and with a ruby like a heart placed in a coronet, with this inscription, *Elizabetha potest*. I durst not do this before I had acquainted you herewith, understanding her Majesty had appointed the masquers, which resolution hath made me the unreadier: yet, if this night I may know her Majesty's leave and your liking, I hope not to come too late, though the time be short for such a show and my preparations posted for such a presence. I desire to come in before the other masque, for I am sorrowful and solemn, and my stay shall not be long. I rest upon your resolution, which must be for this business to-night or not at all.

The letter is only endorsed 'Jan. 1594', but the reference to Lord Derby serves to relate it. Arthur Throgmorton of Paulerspury was brother of Elizabeth Throgmorton, who married Sir Walter Raleigh. But he can hardly have been wishing in 1595 to purge the offence given by his sister in 1592, and of his own marriage I only know that it was to Anne, daughter of Sir John Lucas of Essex (Bridges, *Northamptonshire*, i. 312). Nor can one quite see why he should have intruded his private affairs upon Derby's festival.

This note is growing upon my hands into a dissertation. I must refrain from discussing the troubled early married life of the Stanleys, which justified Bacon's fear that they might 'go to bed fair and rise lowring', rather than Oberon's benediction of 'the best bride-bed'; or the later connexion of the earl with a company of players, which led a quite competent archivist to the astounding discovery that he, another W. S., was the real author of Shakespeare's plays. But I am afraid I must add that I am by no means convinced that *A Midsummer-Night's Dream* was given on 26 January 1595, at all, although the plausibilities are perhaps more in favour of that date than any other.

I should like, however, to be able to explore more fully the circumstances of a wedding which has never yet been considered, that of Thomas, son of Henry Lord Berkeley, and Elizabeth, daughter of Sir George Carey, on 19 February 1596. This is stated in the latest edition of G. E. C.'s peerage, probably on the evidence of the unprinted registers of St. Anne's, to have taken place from the Blackfriars, which is extremely likely, as Sir George Carey had his town house there, next door to the building which became Burbage's Blackfriars theatre. But I do not know that the Queen was present, although she may well have been, as Elizabeth Carey was another of her goddaughters, and granddaughter of her first cousin and Lord Chamberlain, Henry Lord Hunsdon. The attractiveness of the suggestion lies in the fact that Shakespeare's company were Lord Hunsdon's men, and subsequently passed under Sir George Carey's own patronage, when he in his turn became Lord Hunsdon on his father's death later in 1596. Lady Carey was a sister of the Lady Strange to whom *The Tears of the Muses* was dedicated. Sir George Carey is known to have been present at the Elvetham entertainment of 1591, but it would hardly be possible to put the origin of the Berkeley-Carey match there, for it was only in 1595 that this was arranged, after negotiations for Lord Herbert, afterwards Earl of Pembroke, had fallen through, and the Berkeley family chronicler definitely places the beginnings of affection between the young couple in the autumn of that year (Collins, *Sydney Papers*, i. 353, 372; T. Smyth, *Lives of the Berkeleys*, ii. 383, 395).

1916.

THE DATE OF *HAMLET*

I HAVE, in the past, had more occasion than I could have wished, to criticize the writings of Professor J. Dover Wilson on Shakespeare, notably for ascribing to the poet a constant habit of revising his own plays, in which I do not believe, and even sometimes the retention of passages from those of earlier dramatists, used by him as sources. Pausanias tells us how he once visited a temple, in which was a picture by a famous Greek painter of Odysseus in Hades. Among other figures depicted was one of Oknos, condemned eternally to weave a rope of hay, while an ass stood behind him, eating up the rope as fast as he wove it. I have sometimes felt that I stood in the relation of that ass to Professor Wilson. The parallel, no doubt, cuts both ways.

I have, however, much admiration for Professor Wilson's exhaustive work on *Hamlet*, which supplements an edition of the play in 1934, with a two-volume study of *The Manuscript of Shakespeare's Hamlet* in the same year, an *excursus* on *What Happens in Hamlet* in 1935, and some *Corrections and Additional Notes* to the edition in 1936. I am now led, with the help of these, to revise the ascription in my *William Shakespeare* (1930) of the play, as we find it more or less in the Second Quarto and the First Folio, to 1600, and to put it, as Professor Wilson does, in 1601. I had been influenced, unduly as I now think, by a note of Gabriel Harvey in his copy of Speght's *Chaucer* (1598), in which he praises Shakespeare's *Hamlet*, and also records that 'the Earle of Essex much commendes Albions England'. This wording, in the present tense, made me think that the note must have been written before the death of Essex on 25 February 1601, and that, indeed, is the easiest interpretation of it. I do not agree with Professor Wilson that Harvey was writing of an earlier version by Shakespeare of the old dramatic theme of Hamlet, than that which has come down to us, for of any such version I find no other evidence. But I think it is possible, either that 'commendes' is a scribal error for 'commended', or that Harvey had access to some letter or other writing by Essex on *Albion's England*, which has not come down to us. In any case, I do not, on further reflection, think that *Hamlet*, as we have it, can possibly have been written

68

in 1600. The travelling of the 'tragedians of the city' is ascribed (II. ii. 346) to a 'late innovation' which has led to an 'inhibition'. No doubt, an 'innovation' may mean no more than an introduction of a novelty. Shakespeare, however, uses the word or the cognate 'innovator' very rarely, and only in the sense of a political upheaval, or something analogous to that. In *I Henry IV* (v. i. 76) we read of

> poor discontents,
> Which gape and rub the elbow at the news
> Of hurly-burly innovation.

In *Othello* (II. iii. 41) the term is metaphorical, expressing the effect of a cup of drink, 'that was craftily qualified too, and, behold, what innovation it makes here'. In *Coriolanus* (III. i. 175) the tribune, Sicinius, calls Coriolanus,

> a traitorous innovator,
> A foe to the public weal.

I do not now see how the innovation followed by an inhibition of *Hamlet* can well be anything but the outbreak of the Earl of Essex on 8 February 1601. It is true that we have no record of any inhibition ordered by the Privy Council at that time. Possibly one was imposed by the City and local Justices themselves without waiting for instructions. Plays were given at court by the Chapel boys on 22 February and by the Lord Chamberlain's men on 24 February, the eve of Essex's execution. These would not necessarily be affected by any measures taken to prevent popular gatherings in the streets. An order of 11 March 1601 requiring the Chapel and Paul's boys to suspend playing during Lent was merely common form at the penitential season. I do not think that the Chamberlain's play of 24 February can have been *Hamlet*. In that the passage which refers to the travelling of the tragedians of the city, as the result of an inhibition, is followed by another, which states that they had lost estimation through the activity of an aery of children who berattled the common stages and reduced their audience. Poet and player had gone to cuffs in the question, and even Hercules and his load, that is to say the company at the Globe, had suffered. Shakespeare seems here to have dropped the topic of the 'innovation', and to have in mind the general attack upon the common stages in Ben Jonson's *Poetaster*, which was a late outcome of the more personal controversy, already three years old, between Jonson himself and the poets Martson and Dekker, and *Poetaster* can hardly be earlier than the spring of

1601, since in it Histrio declares (III. iv. 328) that 'This
winter ha's made vs all poorer, then so many staru'd snakes'.
Here we have again the inhibition and its financial result to the
players. If then, as seems probable, *Hamlet* shows an aware-
ness of Jonson's baiting of the common stages in *Poetaster*,
Professor Wilson's dating of it in the summer or autumn of
1601 is better than mine. In an 'apologeticall Dialogue' about
Poetaster, spoken at some performance other than the first, and
printed in the Quarto registered on 21 December 1601, Jonson
refers to critics of his play and adds,

> Onely amongst them, I am sorry for
> Some better natures, by the rest so drawne,
> To run in that vile line.

If he is referring to Shakespeare, that might give a final date
for *Hamlet*. But I see no obvious criticism of Jonson, personally, there. Nor do I think that *Hamlet* can be the 'purge',
which, according to the Cambridge writer of the second *Returne from Pernassus*, dating probably from the winter of
1601–2, Shakespeare once gave to Jonson.

I have still, however, to my regret, a little bone to pick with
Professor Wilson. He cites, in confirmation of his date, a sup-
posed reference to a notable episode of contemporary history.
Here he had been anticipated by Dr. G. B. Harrison in his
Last Elizabethan Journal, and his *Shakespeare at Work*, both
of 1933. The theory rests upon the scene (IV. iv), in which a
Norwegian captain, marching through Denmark, in order to
make war on Poland, meets Hamlet, and tells him,

> We go to gain a little patch of ground
> That hath in it no profit but the name.
> To pay five ducats, five, I would not farm it.

Hamlet replies,

> Two thousand souls and twenty thousand ducats
> Will not debate the question of this straw.

And, when left alone, he compares this enterprise for an egg-
shell or a straw with his own irresolution,

>   while to my shame I see
> The imminent death of twenty thousand men,
> That for a fantasy and trick of fame
> Go to their graves like beds, fight for a plot
> Whereon the numbers cannot try the cause,
> Which is not tomb enough and continent
> To hide the slain.

The 'little patch of ground', according to Professor Wilson, was the Dutch town of Ostend, a siege of which by the Archduke Albert of Flanders had begun late in June 1601. And he finds confirmation of this, both in news-pamphlets published in England during its progress, all of which, he says, 'insist upon the insignificance and sterility of the little plot of sandy ground fought for', and in a volume of French poems entitled *Ostende* (B.M. 1192, g.6), and dated in 1603, from one of which he quotes the lines,

> Tout le subiect de ce siege hazardeux
> N'est que ce champ infertile et poudreux.

The poems are apparently by different writers, he tells me, and at least four of them describe the combatants as shedding their blood 'pour un peu de poussière sterile'. He claims, too, in support of his view, the following sentences from an account of the event in Camden's *Elizabeth*,

> There was not in our age any seige and defence maintained with greater slaughter of men, nor continued longer. . . . For the most warlike souldiers of the Low Countreys, Spaine, England, France, Scotland and Italy, whilest they most eagerly contended for a barren plot of sand, had as it were one common sepulcher, but an eternal monument of their valour.

This is, of course, a translation from the Latin of Camden's *Annales*, which runs, in the edition of 1625,

> Nec alia, maiori clade, oppugnatio et propugnatio diutius nostro seculo continuata . . . Bellicosissimis enim ex Belgio, Hispania, Anglia, Gallia, Scotia et Italia viris, dum de sterili arena pugnacissime decertarunt, quasi commune erat sepulchrum, aeternumque virtutis monumentum.

The translator has put the sand into it, but *arena* may mean no more than 'coast'.

I have, unfortunately, not been able, under war conditions, to see the *Ostende* poems, or the full texts of the news-pamphlets. Of these there seem to have been at least five. One (*Short-Title Catalogue* 18893) was registered on 5 August 1601, but had still to be translated from the Dutch before publication. It appears to be this which, according to Professor Wilson, particularly struck Shakespeare's imagination. It describes fighting during July 1601 at a 'place of buriall', which he thinks suggested the 'plot' in *Hamlet*,

> not tomb enough and continent
> To hide the slain.

It was not within Ostend itself, but on high ground, once an old churchyard, outside it. And the pamphlet also contains a mention of the rescue of a man from drowning on a piece of a mast, which Professor Wilson thinks suggested the similar escape of Sebastian in *Twelfth Night* (I. ii). Shakespeare may, no doubt, easily have seen this pamphlet. A second (*S.T.C.* 18894) was apparently published in 1601 without registration. It records events of both July and August in that year. A third (*S.T.C.* 24651), registered on 10 January 1602, describes a parley of 20 December 1601, devised to enable Vere to bring in reinforcements, and a subsequent assault by the Archduke on 28 December. Copies of this were sent by Sir Robert Cecil to two correspondents, shortly after its issue. He says that it came out *sine privilegio*, and notes that 'such is the greediness of printers, as they will never refuse anything that is brought to the press' (*Cal. Hatfield MSS.* xii. 34; xiv. 207–10). Two others (*S.T.C.* 18891 and 18892) were registered on 2 and 25 February 1602 respectively. I do not think that any date later than 1601 can be claimed for *Hamlet*. No doubt all this journalism was eagerly read by Shakespeare, as well as others. Dr. Harrison's summaries of it in his *Last Elizabethan Journal* do not include those constant references to the sterility of the ground, which Professor Wilson seems to have noted.

We are not, of course, wholly dependent upon poems and news-pamphlets for our knowledge of the nature of Ostend in 1601, or of the progress of the siege, which lasted to 24 September 1604. Up to 7 March 1602 the defence of the place was undertaken mainly by English troops, under the command of Sir Francis Vere. Thereafter it passed to the Dutch. An account of the struggle was published by Edward Grimeston in 1604, and others, by Henry Hexham and Sir John Ogle, were appended to William Dillingham's edition of Sir Francis Vere's *Commentaries* in 1657. These can be supplemented from much contemporary material in the *Acts of the Privy Council*, in the *Reports* of the Historical Manuscripts Commission, notably those on Sir Robert Cecil's correspondence at Hatfield (vols. xi, xii, xiv), and Sir Robert Sidney's at Penshurst (vols. ii, iii), in the earlier *Letters and Memorials of State* (1746) of Arthur Collins, also taken from the Penshurst muniments, and in the letters to Cecil from Sir Ralph Winwood at Paris, printed by Edmund Sawyer in his *Memorials of Affairs of State* (1725). Particularly interesting are the numerous 'advices' sent from

time to time by one Captain Holcroft and other officers engaged in the defence, and preserved at Hatfield. Naturally
many of the documents here described were of a confidential
nature, although something of the information conveyed may
have been allowed to leak out from them. The Hatfield papers
include (xi. 293, 354, 583; xiv. 305) no less than five plans of
Ostend, taken during the siege, but unfortunately none of these
have been reproduced. It is possible, however, from the
material available, to get some conception of the lay-out of the
area, which must of course, in 1601, have been matter of
general knowledge. Ostend, on the coast of Zeeland, which
here runs from the south-west to the north-east, was an out-
lying stronghold of the Dutch States, and only accessible, either
from their towns farther north or from England, by sea. It
stood on sandy ground, and was backed by high dunes, from
which the rather ineffective artillery of the age could annoy it.
On these the Archduke had set up a ring of small forts, called
sconces. One of these, on the south-west, lay behind a small
river. On the Ostend side of it was a 'polder' of low-lying land
reclaimed from the sea. But the most important feature of
Ostend was the old haven towards the north-east. It was not
a very good one, especially in rough weather, and was approached by a narrow entrance, called the Geule. So long as
this could be kept open, reinforcements from England could
be got in, and the task of the besiegers remained difficult. By
the end of 1601 it had suffered, and Vere began the construction of a new haven beyond it. This was risky, as it might let
water into the inhabited area, which stood further back, but
still on low ground. Here was an old town, with a church, and
apparently a new town had grown up towards the west as a
suburb. There was a good deal of fortification. We read of
bulwarks. Two of these, a Sandhills and a Poulter, apparently
named from the 'polder', were both in the old town. There
were also a Helmont and a Peck's bulwark. There were half-
moons, bastions, curtains, counterscarps, and ravelins. One
ravelin was called the porcupine (porkupie, porcpie, porcke-
pey, porcespy). The *Oxford Dictionary* defines this as 'a machine
with projecting spikes or teeth', but here it appears to have
been something more substantial.

I do not see how such a locality could be described, even by
a poet, as 'a little patch of ground' or as 'a plot whereon the
numbers cannot try the cause', or as merely a straw to be

debated. Hamlet, incidentally, says nothing about the presence of sand in the plot. And, of course, it is not true that Ostend had 'in it no profit but the name'. There is abundant contemporary evidence of its value to the Dutch, both as an avenue for trade and as a link with their English ally. On the other hand, so long as it was unconquered, it remained a thorn in the side of the Archduke. Vere himself wrote to the Privy Council on 28 June 1601 of the Dutch (*Cal. Hatfield MSS.* xi. 253),

> They are not a little troubled, the town being to them of such importance, as in a manner their whole welfare depends upon the conservation thereof.

And he adds,

> I cannot forbear to utter what is thought here the loss of that place would bring with it. First, all the hope of clearing that coast is taken away, the enemy's means to annoy us by sea trebled, he is eased of an infinite charge the blocking that place required, and his revenue by the quieting of that quarter much increased, and this conclusion is drawn out, that the enemy in short time will disjoint this state, without striking an offensive blow by land, if they be not more helped by their neighbours than yet there is any appearance of. On the other side it may please your Honours to understand what is conceived if this succours of her Majesty's arrive in time: that it will be the utter ruin of the enemy if he be obstinate, and of Flanders, either by his own forces or ours, what course soever he take.

So, too, on 10 July 1601, one William Tresham, who wanted employment by Cecil, wrote to a friend of Ostend, as 'a place of most importance for the States of Holland to continue and possess', and of the Archduke (*Cal. Hatfield MSS.* xi. 280),

> Sure, if he become master of the place, he will be much esteemed: so contrariwise, if he fail of the enterprise, he will not only lose much reputation, but withal will be put to great afterdeal and distress.

To Cecil himself Captain Richard Wigmore reported of the Dutch on 11 August 1601 (*Cal. Hatfield MSS.* xi. 336),

> They will engage themselves far beyond ordinary, rather than yield to the loss of Ostend. It undoubtedly carryeth with it matter of greater consequence than any other that hath fallen out for a long time in these parts, for if the Archduke faileth in this project, he must, in all likelihood, seek himself elsewhere than in Flanders; but if Ostend be lost, it is more clear than the sun that all the towns in Zealand will be transformed into villages, if they be not utterly abandoned.

From another angle we get the Spanish view of the position, summed up in what seems to be an intercepted communication of 3 September 1601 (*Cal. Hatfield MSS.* xi. 380). 'In short, the necessity of winning this town is great, for otherwise the estate of these Princes will be desperate.' Sir Ralph Winwood, describing an interview on 12 October 1601 with Henri IV at Paris, in which he had told him of Elizabeth's preoccupation with the affairs of Ireland, adds that he had said (E. Sawyer, *Memorials of Affairs of State*, i. 354),

That which gave her the greatest discontent was, that hereby her peculiar desseignes wer somewhat disturbed, and her means and thoughts detourned from the assistance of the States; whose necessity she knowes to be great, and without the greater providence of God, and succours from him, doth presage a great alteration in their fortunes. I then remonstrated [? demonstrated] to him (insisting from point to point upon those particulars which your Honor hath set down) the deplorable state of Ostend, and recommended from her Majestie unto his care the protection of that towne; which it might please him to have in so much the more particuler recommendation, in that the wellfare of their fortunes did depend upon the issue of this siege: which I shewed, both that the Archduke should be greatly advanced in reputation by gaining that towne; and more in estate, by reducing all Flanders into a peaceable possession; and the Hollander's commerce (which is the Peru of their finances) by the loss of that porte, in a manner ruinated, or much impeached.

And we have a final confirmation from Cecil himself, on 28 January 1602 (*Cal. Hatfield MSS.* xii. 34).

But we must not desist. For if we can still engage and waste that army, which is the garland of Spain, before that place, he will be at little ease to think of other enterprises; it being sufficient reason for us to value that port at a high price, seeing he could be contented to purchase it at so dear a rate.

A high price, not the five ducats, at which the Norwegian captain told Hamlet he would not farm the little patch of ground, he was marching to gain.

1943.

THE INTEGRITY OF *THE TEMPEST*

DISINTEGRATING criticism has approached the problem of *The Tempest* by four paths.

1. There are certain analogies to the play in *Die Schöne Sidea*, which forms part of the *Opus Theatricum* (1618) of Jacob Ayrer of Nuremberg (*ob.* 1605). Here, as in *The Tempest*, we find a prince and magician, with a familiar spirit, a fair daughter, and an enemy's son, whose sword is held in thrall by the magician's art, who must bear logs for the lady, and who wins release through her love. Such a task and its solution form a common enough theme of romance and folk-tale, from Theseus and Ariadne onwards. The resources of *Quellen-forschung* have been fully equal to tracing it in Renaissance, especially Spanish, literature. The details of the logs and the stayed sword probably point to some closer community of origin between *Sidea* and *The Tempest*. It should perhaps be added that the enemy of Ayrer's magician has a councillor Franciscus, and in *The Tempest* a Francisco has a rather shadowy existence, apparently as a 'lord' of the usurping duke of Milan. The stage-directions note his entries at II. i. 1, III. iii. 1, v. i. 58; but he only speaks three words at III. iii. 40, and ten lines at II. i. 113, which very probably really belong to Gonzalo. It has been thought that Ayrer used a pre-1605 version of *The Tempest* as a model. But obviously other explanations are equally plausible; a knowledge by Shakespeare of the German play, or of a report of it brought home by English actors from Germany; a common source, dramatic or narrative, now lost. This might be the *Celinde und Sedea* found in Anglo-German play-lists of 1604 and 1613, although no name resembling Celinde is in Ayrer's play. Certainly, as we have them, *The Tempest* and *Sidea* are distinct plays. They have very different local and historical settings. *Sidea* has no storm and no magic island. And there are no parallels of phrase, such as would suggest a common archetypal text. It is true that in the new Cambridge edition of *The Tempest* (1921) Sir A. Quiller-Couch tells us (p. xlix) 'that "mountain" and "silver", two names of the spirit hounds which Prospero and Ariel set upon the "foul conspiracy" (IV. i. 256), occur in an invocation of Prince Ludolph's in the German play', and that his colleague, Mr. J. D. Wilson, says more

cautiously (p. 104) that 'there is an obscure mention of "silver, hill and mountain" in *Die Schöne Sidea* which may refer to spirits'. But there is surely some misunderstanding here. The phrase does not occur in an invocation of Ludolph's at all, and I cannot find anything obscure or any reference to spirits in it. It is in a speech by Sidea's rival Julia, to whom there is no analogue in *The Tempest*. Julia is describing her reception by her prospective father-in-law (not the magician Ludolph, but his enemy, Leudegast), and says, 'Verheist mir Silber Hügel vnd Berg'. It is simple enough. The silver and land were her promised dower.

2. It has been held that the fragment of a mask in IV. i. is an interpolation into the play as originally written, and by some that it is not Shakespeare's work, but Beaumont's or Chapman's. The motive is supposed to have been a desire to adapt the play to the circumstances of the winter season of 1612–13, which preceded the wedding of the Princess Elizabeth and Frederick the Elector Palatine, on 14 February 1613. No doubt *The Tempest* is recorded to have been given at court on some unnamed day during this season, and the appropriateness of the hymeneal mask is evident. But we do not know that it was not equally appropriate to the earlier performance which is also recorded on 1 November 1611, and which may also have celebrated, although we do not know that it did celebrate, some courtly wedding. There is only one specific reference in the mask itself which can yield a clue (IV. i. 114):

> Spring come to you at the farthest
> In the very end of harvest!

Mr. Dover Wilson tells us that '"Spring" here is clearly a veiled reference to the "offspring" of the royal marriage (cf. "issue", l. 105), since nine months from the beginning of 1613 takes us to "the very end of harvest".' I dare say it does, but the royal marriage was on 14 February, and even if we accept Mr. W. J. Lawrence's rather arbitrary conjecture (*Fortnightly*, cxiii. 941) that the play was given at the betrothal on 27 December, it would hardly be decent, in view of what Prospero says about 'bed-right', to start the calculation from that day. As a matter of fact, the allusion fits the 1611 performance well enough, since the words 'at the farthest' allow a little margin over nine months.

3. Mr. Dover Wilson makes use of points 1 and 2, although

he does not commit himself upon, and oddly enough does not discuss, the authorship of the mask. In other respects, however, he carries the critical analysis a good deal further. He disclaims an attempt 'to frame a hypothetical history of *The Tempest* MS.'. But he finds 'good reason to suppose that the "copy" for the Folio text was author's manuscript which had served as prompt-copy in the theatre', lays down the general principle that 'prompt-copy in that age might have a long history', and thinks that 'the condition of the Folio text appears to show that *The Tempest* MS. had seen many changes before it reached the printer's hands'. Becoming more specific, he makes the following suggestions:

(i) 'When Shakespeare took up *The Tempest* late in his career he had an old manuscript to go upon, possibly an early play of his own, which may have been related to the original of *Die Schöne Sidea*.' This view is based upon (*a*) traces of cancelled rhymed couplets, and (*b*) a scrap of doggerel, both of which Mr. Wilson regards as signs of early work.

(ii) 'The received text has been clearly abridged, and abridged in the main by Shakespeare himself', and in I. ii. 187–320 (Prospero's first dialogue with Ariel, containing the exposition of Caliban's prehistory) 'the abridgement is distinctly cruder and more drastic than elsewhere'. The proof of this consists of (*a*) the shortness of the play; (*b*) broken lines, taken as indicating 'cuts'; (*c*) incorrect verse-lining, taken as indicating marginal alterations; (*d*) unsystematic mingling of verse and prose; (*e*) incomplete or inconsistent handling of minor characters; (*f*) the immense length of the second scene. It requires, perhaps, some ingenuity to turn the length of a scene into an argument for abridgement. But Mr. Wilson explains that most of the second scene 'is taken up with an account of events which we may assume provided material for pre-wreck scenes in the earlier version'; and goes on to point to the 'remarkable' fact that the early scenes of *The Tempest* contain three separate expositions. 'The threefold difficulty is tackled by Shakespeare with consummate skill; but the expositions are there, and they tell their own tale. At some stage of its evolution *The Tempest* was in all likelihood a loosely constructed drama, like *A Winter's Tale* and *Pericles*.'

(iii) 'The Masque, which we can with certainty date early 1613 or Christmas 1612, appears to be an after-thought inserted into Act 4 when the play had already taken final shape under Shakespeare's hand', and it was perhaps the need to make room for this addition, whether carried out by Shakespeare or another, which led to the crude abridgement of i. ii. 187–320.

If then I understand Mr. Wilson aright, there have been two distinct abridgements, not necessarily for the same production; firstly a general abridgement, entailing the replacement of pre-wreck scenes by expositions, and leaving the play as a whole short, but the second scene immense; and then a further abridgement, to enable the mask-scene (iv. i) to be expanded without adding to the total length of the play. I will return shortly to an analysis, through several scenes, of Mr. Wilson's evidence.

4. Mr. H. D. Gray, in 'Some Indications that *The Tempest* was Revised' (1921, *Studies in Philology*, xviii. 129), points out that Act iv, as it stands, would be empty without the mask, and, while accepting this as an insertion, suggests that it replaced matter in which the plots of Caliban and Stephano against Prospero and of Anthonio and Sebastian against Alonso received greater elaboration. This is conceivable, although I do not think that either intrigue is demonstrably incomplete, or could have been carried much further against the omnipotence of Prospero. No doubt the Anthonio theme is left sketchy and rather unmotived, but its dramatic purpose is served in adding a touch of black to the character of Anthonio. The Caliban plot is of course mere farce, and ends happily enough in the 'filthy mantled pool'. It is not, and never could have been, serious enough quite to explain Prospero's passion at the mask. The mask, however, had to be broken off abruptly, in order to obviate the necessity of staging the full teams of dancers. The masks brought into plays are rarely completed. Mr. Gray partly rests his case upon the use of the motive of stealing the magician's books in *Li Tre Satiri*, one of a group of Italian *scenari*, which he supposes (1920, 'The Sources of the *Tempest*', in *Modern Language Notes*, xxxv. 321) to be the origin of the play. These *scenari* were printed by F. Neri, *Scenari delle Maschere in Arcadia* (1913), from the large collection made by Basilio Locatelli and now in the Casanatense at Rome. Unfortunately, this book is now out of print, and so far I have not been able to trace a copy in this country. To judge by Mr. Gray's description, a number of episodes, spread over half a dozen *scenari*, do in the aggregate bear such a resemblance to

the theme of *The Tempest* as to suggest some kind of connexion. But what that connexion was remains obscure. Locatelli's manuscript is dated 1622, according to Mr. Gray, 1618 according to a reviewer in the *Athenaeum* (20 March 1915). Obviously there is no evidence here of priority to *The Tempest*. On the other hand, the *scenari* might relate to performances of earlier date than that of the manuscript. Mr. Gray says that 'there is no reason to doubt that Shakespeare could have seen them acted in London'. The plausibility of this depends upon whether they *were* acted in London, and surely this is a hazardous conjecture as regards any particular group of seventeenth-century Italian *scenari*. Visits of Italian actors to this country were not very frequent. The only early Jacobean example known to me, and unfortunately overlooked in writing Chapter XIV of *The Elizabethan Stage*, was in 1610, when Prince Henry's privy purse accounts (*S.P. Dom. Jac. I*, lvii. 87) show payments to 'an Italian comedian' of £5 on 17 March and £2 on 13 April. On 9 January Henry gave £6 to 'Daniell the Italian'. He is not called a comedian, and I cannot trace an actor of that name in the *Accesi* or *Fedeli* or any other known Italian troupe.

I now turn to the play itself. And first for the stage-directions. These are more elaborate than in any other play of the canon, and have sometimes been thought to be the work of a Folio editor for the assistance of readers. I agree, however, with Mr. Wilson that they may very well be substantially due to Shakespeare himself, writing in absence from London, and anxious to replace his personal supervision by careful instructions on apparel and stage-business to the producer. If so, they do not militate against the view that *The Tempest* was printed from prompt-copy. On the other hand, the mere presence of author's directions does not of itself prove this, and I am not quite sure what are Mr. Wilson's reasons for supposing that the copy used for the Folio had in fact served as prompt-copy. He does not point to anything clearly due to a book-keeper as distinct from a playwright. I think, however, that there are in fact some faint indications of certain alterations in the interests of *spectacle*, for which Shakespeare was probably not responsible. I shall come to these in due course. My quotations are from the Globe text, except where any purpose is served by keeping the orthography or punctuation of the Folio.

ACT I, SCENE I (*The Wreck Scene*)

This is written in alternating sections of prose and verse. Mr. Wilson regards this as evidence of revision, and thinks that it was 'probably a verse-scene in the original unrevised play'. To me the alternation appears intentional and dramatic; the emotional tone rising and falling with the fits of the storm. The more excited passages, including the boatswain's cries to the mariners, are in verse, often rough and broken; during the lulls the boatswain and the courtiers exchange comments and abuse in prose. This arrangement has misled the compositor, who prints far too much as prose, and incidentally, after the Folio fashion, tends to elide syllables which are required by the scansion. To some extent this is admitted by Mr. Wilson, who recovers seven verse-lines, 'partly by expanding contractions'. I should go farther, and arrange as follows (the brackets indicate elisions or omissions of the Folio):

A tempestuous noise of Thunder and Lightning heard: Enter a Ship-master, and a Boteswaine.

Master	Bote-swaine.
Boteswaine	Heere Master: What cheere?
Mast.	Good: Speake to th[e] Mariners: fall too [i]t, yarely, Or we run our selues a ground, bestirre, bestirre.

Enter Mariners.

Botes.	Heigh my hearts, cheerely, cheerely my harts: yare, yare: Take in the toppe-sale: Tend to th[e] Masters whistle: Blow till thou burst thy winde, if roome enough.

Enter Alonso, Sebastian, Anthonio, Ferdinando, Gonzalo, and others.

ALONSO	Good Boteswaine haue [a ?] care: where [i]s the Master? Play the men.
Botes.	I pray now keepe below.
Anthonio	Where is the Master, Boson?
Botes.	Do you not heare him? you marre our labour, Keepe your Cabines: you do assist the storme.
Gonzalo	Nay, good be patient.
Botes.	When the Sea is: hence, What cares these roarers for the name of King? To Cabine; silence: trouble us not.
Gon.	Good, yet remember whom thou hast aboord.
Botes.	None that I more loue then my selfe. You are a Counsellor, if you can command these Elements to silence, and worke the peace of the present, wee will not hand a rope more,

vse your authoritie: If you cannot, giue thankes you haue
liu'd so long, and make your selfe readie in your Cabine for
the mischance of the houre, if it so hap.

Cheerely good hearts: out of our way I say.   *Exit.*

Gon.   I haue great comfort from this fellow: methinks he hath no
drowning marke vpon him, his complexion is perfect Gal-
lowes: stand fast good Fate to his hanging, make the rope
of his destiny our cable, for our owne doth little aduantage:
If he be not borne to bee hang'd, our case is miserable.

Exit.

Enter Boteswaine.

Botes.   Downe with the top-Mast: yare, lower, lower,
Bring her to Try with Maine-course.
A plague——

A cry within. Enter Sebastian, Anthonio and Gonzalo.
vpon this howling:
They are lowder then the weather, or our office:
Yet againe? What do you heere? Shal we giue ore and
drowne, haue you a minde to sinke?

Seb.   A poxe o' your throat, you bawling, blasphemous incharitable
Dog.

Botes.   Worke you then.

Anth.   Hang cur, hang, you whoreson insolent Noyse-maker, we are
lesse afraid to be drownde, then thou art.

Gonz.   I'le warrant him for drowning, though the Ship were no
stronger then a Nutt-shell, and as leaky as an vnstanched
wench.

Botes.   Lay her a hold, a hold, set her two courses
Off to Sea againe, lay her off.

Enter Mariners wet.

Mari.   All lost, to prayers, to prayers, all lost.

Botes.   What must our mouths be cold?

Gonz.   The King, and Prince, at prayers, let's assist them,
For our case is as theirs.

Seb.   I'am out of patience.

Anth.   We are meerly cheated of our liues by drunkards,
This wide-chopt-rascall, would thou mightst lye drowning
The washing of ten Tides.

Gonz.   Hee'l be hang'd yet,
Though euery drop of water sweare against it,
And gape at widst to glut him.   *A confused noyse within.*
Mercy on vs
We split, we split. Farewell my wife, and children,
Farewell brother: we split, we split, we split.

Anth.	Let's all sinke wi['] th[e] King.
Seb.	Let's take leaue of him. *Exit.*
Gonz.	Now would I giue a thousand furlongs of Sea, for an Acre of barren ground: Long heath, Browne firrs, any thing; the wills aboue be done, but I would faine dye a dry death.

Exit.

Of the thirty-four lines here treated as verse, only six are so treated by the Folio and twenty-two by Mr. Wilson. I must add that the verse does not read to me at all like early work of Shakespeare.

ACT I, SCENE II

1–186 (*Prospero and Miranda: the First Exposition*).
    Only two passages require comment.

(*a*) Prospero tells Miranda that she knows no more than that he is Prospero and her father. She says (21):

> More to know
> Did never meddle with my thoughts,

but in her very next speech (33)

> You have often
> Begun to tell me what I am, but stopp'd,
> And left me to a bootless inquisition,
> Concluding, 'Stay: not yet.'

This is one of those small inconsistencies of dialogue which are frequent in Shakespeare, pass easily on the stage, and must not be pressed as evidence for revision.

(*b*) 156–60:

Pros.	which raised in me
	An undergoing stomach, to bear up
	Against what should ensue.
Mir.	How came we ashore?
Pros.	By providence divine,
	Some food, we had, and some fresh water, that
	A noble Neapolitan, Gonzalo . . . did give us . . .

Mr. Wilson comments: 'The isolated half-line and the comma suggest a "cut" here. Prospero never answers Miranda's question.' But he does. They came ashore, because Providence, acting through Gonzalo, had supplied them with food and water. As for the half-line, it is common enough for a half-line speech, breaking into a longer speech, to do double duty as a member of two successive metrical lines.

187–320 (*Prospero and Ariel: the Second Exposition*).

Mr. Wilson finds 'bibliographical disturbance', from which he infers 'cuts' and insertions, concentrated in this section of the scene.

(*a*) There are five broken lines:

(188)   Approach, my Ariel, come.   *Enter Ariel.*
(316)   Come, thou tortoise! when?
                                        Enter Ariel like a water nymph.

            Thou poisonous slave, got by the devil himself
(320)   Upon thy wicked dam, come forth!   *Enter Caliban.*

Two (188, 320) are speech-endings, at the other (316) the speaker turns to a new addressee; and in all these cases entries fill the pauses.

    Pros.   Hast thou, spirit,
            Perform'd to point the tempest that I bade thee?
(195) *Ariel.* To every article.
            I boarded the king's ship, now on the beak . . .

This is rather abrupt, but Ariel may take pause to think before he begins his story. Little, if anything, can be missing, since the twelve lines of Ariel's speech fully answer Prospero's question.

            Thou dost, and think'st it much to tread the ooze
(253)   Of the salt deep,
            To run upon the sharp wind of the north,
            To do me business in the veins o' th' earth
            When it is baked with frost.

This is certainly abrupt. Mr. Wilson calls it a 'glaring cut'. Dr. Greg (*M.L.R.* xvii. 178) points out that the speech runs too smoothly for a mere cut, and thinks that there may have been a more substantial alteration, from a passage containing a line

            Think'st much to tread the ooze of the salt deep,

But again there cannot be much missing: the dialogue as a whole is consistent and adequate.

    As a matter of fact, there is a sixth broken line, which Mr. Wilson does not note:

                            they all have met again,
            And are upon the Mediterranean flote,
(235)   Bound sadly home for Naples,
            Supposing that they saw the King's ship wracked,
            And his great person perish.

The completeness of the grammatical structure makes any substantial cut unlikely.

(*b*) The lineation of the Folio, as throughout the play, is good, but there is one mis-division (309–10), where

> *Mir.* 'Tis a villain, sir, I do not love to look on.—

contains the end of one line and the beginning of the next. I think the Folio has a tendency to merge consecutive half-lines, for the saving of space.

(*c*) Mr. Wilson finds the account of Sycorax in Argier (260–7) obscure, and thinks that a fuller narrative has been cut. Certainly we are left in doubt as to whether the witch was born in Argier and why her life was spared. I doubt whether there is anything in this but the awkwardness due to the attempt (noticeable also in 1–186) to break the exposition by question and answer.

(*d*) Mr. Wilson thinks that the account of Caliban (281–6), which breaks into the story of Ariel's imprisonment and release, is 'an addition, a piece of patchwork, designed to compensate for a rent elsewhere in this section'. Dr. Greg apparently agrees. Here also I find nothing but rather clumsy exposition.

Both Mr. Wilson and Dr. Greg also find 'botchery' in the following, where 'correct lining and scansion are impossible, and the repetition of the prefix *Pro.* points to a join in the MS.

(298) *Pro.* Doe so: and after two daies
  I will discharge thee.
  Ar. That's my noble Master:
  What shall I doe? say what? what shall I doe?
  Pro. Goe make thy selfe like a Nymph o' th' Sea,
  Be subject to no sight but thine, and mine: inuisible
  To euery eye-ball else: goe take this shape
  And hither come in't: goe: hence
  With diligence.   *Exit.*
  Pro. Awake, deere hart awake, thou hast slept well,
  Awake.

I am inclined to agree that there has been an insertion, not as part of a recast of the scene, but at the hands of the book-keeper, to lead up to an elaboration of the spectacular element in the play by the momentary and dramatically purposeless apparition of Ariel '*like a water nymph*' at l. 316 (*v. supra*). If so, of course the broken line (316) may after all be part of the alteration.

321–74 (*Prospero and Caliban*).

(*a*) Mr. Wilson finds three broken lines:

> A south-west blow on ye,
> (324)   And blister you all o'er.

A broken line at the end of a speech in a late play is common enough, and no proof of a cut.

> *Pros.*   thou didst seek to violate
> (348)   The honour of my child.
> *Cal.*   O ho, O ho! would't had been done.

Here we have, not two broken lines, but one complete one. Caliban's laugh is extra-metrical.

(*b*) The Folio (360–2) reads:

> therefore wast thou
> Deseruedly confin'd into this Rocke, who hadst
> Deseru'd more then a prison.

Mr. Wilson redivides:

> Deservedly confined into this rock,
> Who hadst deserved more than a prison.

And he comments, 'The rough verse, the broken line and the echo "deservedly . . . deserved" all suggest hasty revision.' I do not know that his four and a half foot line is any less 'rough' than the six footer. If I were given to emendation, I think I should assume that 'deseru'd' had caught the compositor's eye twice, and let it run, still with a broken speech ending:

> Confin'd into this rock, who hadst deserved
> More than a prison.

In any case, the passage looks to me like a misprint, rather than a revision.

376–501 (*Prospero, Ferdinand, and Miranda*).

Mr. Wilson finds 'no bibliographical peculiarities'; neither do I, except a final broken line (501).

ACT II, SCENE 1

1–190 (*The Third Exposition: Gonzalo's Philosophy*).

Prose and verse are a good deal mixed, and a verse line or two may be embedded in prose passages. Mr. Wilson takes the prose for a revision; but such a piecemeal revision wants as much explanation as an original mixture. Certainly the verse, which on the whole is used for the more exalted passages, is not early work.

191–327 (*Plot against Alonso*).

(*a*) Mr. Wilson does not note two broken lines, one (218) a speech-ending, the other (275) an exclamation.

(*b*) There are three cases of misdivided lines (192–3, 195–8, 244–5), but sporadic misdivisions are very poor evidence of revision, and Mr. Wilson's attempt at a reconstruction of an original form for 192–8 suggests that, if there was any revision, it was quite trivial. In 244–5 I only see space-saving, analogous to that of i. ii. 309–10.

(*c*) In 297–305 Ariel enters and sings a song in Gonzalo's ear. This seems inconsistent with the conversation after the waking of Alonso and Gonzalo (in itself intelligible enough, *pace* Mr. Wilson), in which Gonzalo speaks of a 'humming' and the disturbed murderers of a 'bellowing' or 'roare'. Possibly the song, like i. ii. 298–305, may be a theatrical sophistication.

ACT II, SCENE II (*Caliban and Mariners*)

The mariners speak prose; Caliban mainly, but not entirely, verse. The Folio compositor, as in i. i, is confused, prints some of Caliban's lines as prose, and contrariwise has some irregular prose lines with initial capitals. Mr. Wilson thinks that this is the result of revision, but original differentiation, to emphasize the abnormality of Caliban, is just as plausible as differentiated revision.

ACT III, SCENE I (*Ferdinand and Miranda*)

Mr. Wilson (p. 84) finds 'no marks of revision', but (p. 79) notes certain traces of rhymed couplets as indicating Shakespeare's use of 'an old manuscript, possibly an early play of his own'. These are:

(24)   I'll bear your logs the while: pray give me that;
         I'll carry it to the pile.
(29)   I should do it
         With much more ease: for my good will is to it,

Mere carelessness, I think.

ACT III, SCENE II (*Caliban and Mariners*)

The arrangement is similar to that of ii. ii, except that occasionally Stephano, as well as Caliban, speaks verse. Trinculo has three lines, probably of doggerel (86–9), although treated by the Globe as prose, which Mr. Wilson thinks 'fossil from the earlier version'.

ACT III, SCENE III

Mr. Wilson finds 'marks of revision, slight'. These appear to be:

(*a*) Four broken lines, of which one (19) is a short exclamatory speech, and three (52, 82, 93) are speech-endings, the first two being cut short by thunder.

(*b*) One misdivision, due, I think, like I. ii. 309–10, to the merging of what would normally appear as two half-lines in the Folio.

	Ant.	Doe not for one repulse forgoe the purpose
(13)		That you resolu'd t'effect.
	Seb.	The next aduantage will we take throughly.
	Ant.	Let it be to night,

(*c*) Two buried rhymes, analogous to III. i. 24.

(32)	Their manners are more gentle-kind, than of
	Our human generation you shall find
	Many, nay, almost any.
(50)	Although my last: no matter, since I feele
	The best is past.

ACT IV, SCENE I

1–193 (*The Mask Scene*).

(*a*) One misdivision, clearly to save space.

(166) *Pro.*   Spirit: We must prepare to meet with Caliban.

(*b*) Seven broken lines, of which one (43) is an independent speech, followed by a change to trochaic metre, three (12, 105, 169) are speech-endings, and three, also speech-endings (59, 127, 138), are cut short by appearances of the mask. Mr. Wilson does not note 12 and 43, and accepts the others as due to 'the exigencies of the masque-verse'.

What then is the evidence for the mask being an interpolation?

(i) I have already shown that the obstetric chronology has no necessary or obvious relation to the circumstances of 1612–13.

(ii) Mr. Wilson thinks that an earlier version of the play only had the dances of Reapers and Nymphs (138), and that the speeches and song of Iris, Ceres, and Juno (60–138), together with the preliminary talk of Prospero with Ariel and Ferdinand

(48–59), have been added. He argues that all this intermediate matter is inconsistent with Prospero's 'incite them to quick motion' (39) and 'Ay: with a twink' (43), and with Ariel's words (46–7):

> Each one, tripping on his toe,
> Will be here with mop and mow.—

'which announce the immediate advent of dancers'. This seems to me fantastic literalism, even if it can be assumed that Iris and Ceres and Juno did not themselves come in with dancing measures. Mr. Wilson goes on to explain the introduction of the intermediate matter, with its second and rather superfluous moral warning to Ferdinand, as due to the fact that Ariel 'presented Ceres' (167), and therefore the actor of Ariel needed time to change his costume. As to this Dr. Greg points out that, whatever Ariel says, the parts were not necessarily doubled by the human actors; to which I may add, that 'presented' need mean no more than that Ariel stage-managed the show. I do not therefore see any evidence of patching before the mask. According to the usual practice in such entertainments, speaking personages introduce the dancers. And, although I agree that the second sermon to Ferdinand is clumsy, the rest of the preliminary matter fits well enough. Ariel is told to get ready quickly, and then told (49) to delay the actual entry until Prospero gives the word; which in fact he does at 57.

(iii) Is there, then, any more convincing proof of patching after the mask? Again Mr. Wilson applies his wardrobe argument. Ariel must change his dress again, and so Prospero, although he has stopped the mask in order to be getting quickly to grips with the dangerous Caliban conspiracy, has to delay for thirteen lines of 'irrelevant philosophical rhapsody' about the 'insubstantial pageant' of life. Mr. Wilson suggests that in the original version Prospero's (158) 'Sir, I am vexed' was a direct reply to Ferdinand's

(143)   This is strange: your father's in some passion
            That works him strongly.

This, however, would not give a complete line at the juncture, and Dr. Greg reconstructs the dialogue as follows:

> *Ferd.* You do look, my lord, in a moved sort
>   As if you were dismayed.
> *Pros.*   Sir, I am vexed.

My own conviction is that these critics take Prospero's

'passion' and the danger of the Caliban conspiracy much more seriously than Prospero did, that the mask was stopped because there had been enough of it for the purposes of a play, and that there has been no patching. If there has, Shakespeare's undeniable authorship of the 'insubstantial pageant' passage makes the conclusion that he was the patcher inevitable.

Interpolation, if it could be shown, would however strengthen the hands of those who doubt the Shakespearean workmanship of the mask itself; from the old Cambridge editors with their unspecific reference to 'the writer who composed the masque' to Dr. Greg, who says that it is in 'a very distinctive style, quite different from Shakespeare's'. Fleay ascribed it to Beaumont, in whose wedding mask of 1613 Iris and the Naiades again appear. In *The Tempest* the Naiades have 'sedged crowns' and Ceres has 'banks with pioned and twilled brims'. In the wedding mask were 'four delicate fountains, running with water and bordered with sedges and water-flowers'. This is extraordinarily thin. Iris, the messenger of the Gods, and the Naiades show no recondite imagination in a mask-writer. They might well serve twice in a season; it is less probable that the same writer would use them twice in the same season. Nor is it odd that two masks with nuptial themes should both allude to 'blessing and increase'. Mr. J. M. Robertson (*Shakespeare and Chapman*, 210; *Times Literary Supplement*, 31 March 1921) offers as alternatives Heywood, who is not likely to have written for the King's men, and Chapman, with a leaning towards Chapman, indicated by the bad rhyming, by word-clues, and by the duplication of Juno's mention of 'honour' and 'riches' in Chapman's own wedding mask, in which 'Honour' and 'Plutus (or Riches)' are in fact characters. It is suggested that Chapman had already seen Beaumont's mask and took from this some details of imagery; also that he had already seen *The Tempest*, of which there are some echoes in his wedding mask, and took from II. i. 163 the word 'foison' for the interpolated mask. It is, however, to the word-clues that Mr. Robertson devotes most attention. He finds in *The Tempest* mask eighteen words (vetches, turfy, stover, pioned, twilled, brims, betrims, broom-groves, lorn, marge, bosky, unshrubb'd, bed-right, windring, sedged, sicklemen, furrow, rye-straw) not used elsewhere by Shakespeare, and eight words or phrases (donation, crisp, leas, scandal'd, many colour'd messenger, scarcity, sunburnt, dusky), which Shakespeare only uses two or three times, sometimes in plays in which Mr. Robertson thinks that Chapman or another had a hand. Of the first group he traces three (brims, bed-rites, furrow) and of the second four (leas, scandal'd, sunburnt, dusky), together with, not 'many-colour'd', but 'thousand-colour'd', as an epithet of Iris, in Chapman. 'This', he says, 'does not amount to much.' It certainly does not, in view of the commonplace character of many of the words and the frequency of once-used words in all Shakespeare's plays. It is therefore a little surprising to find Mr. Robertson reverting to the matter and telling us (*T.L.S.*) that the vocabulary clues to Chapman are 'rather striking'. Such as it is, the case must be further discounted by pointing out that 'brim' occurs, not once, but four times in the plays, and that 'furrow' as a noun recurs in the compound 'furrow-weeds'. Nor is it helped by pointing out that coupled epithets and such forms as 'turfy', 'bosky', are very much in Chapman's manner, since they are also very much in Shakespeare's. And it is rather misleading to suggest that 'spongy April' recalls the 'Earth, at this spring, spongy and languorsome' of Chapman's *Amorous Zodiac*, without also noting the 'spongy south' of *Cymbeline* IV. ii. 349. Iris rhymes 'deity' with 'society', and Chapman in the wedding mask with 'piety', but in neither case is an abnormal pronunciation of 'deity' involved; the rhyme is only on the last syllable.

Looking at the matter more broadly, I do not think it possible to read the dialogue of the mask side by side with Beaumont's elegant wedding mask, or Chapman's extremely cumbrous one, and to believe in any common authorship with either of them. That is an issue, not of analogies of motive, or of word-clues, but of stylistic impression, of which each critic must be the judge for himself. Nor do I see any reason to doubt that this dialogue is Shakespeare's. Certainly its manner is differentiated from that of the play itself; it had to be pitched in a different key, just as the play in *Hamlet* is pitched in a different key from that of *Hamlet* itself. But why should we look for another than Shakespeare in the 'banks with pioned and twilled brims', in the 'spongy April' and the 'cold nymphs', in the 'rich scarf to my proud earth', in 'Mars' hot minion', and the 'blind boy's scandal'd company'; above all, in the turn of

> thy broom-groves,
> Whose shadow the dismissed bachelor loves,
> Being lass-lorn?

About the song of Juno and Ceres, with its imperfect rhymes and its emptiness of content, I feel more doubtful; and if any one argues that this, taken by itself, may have been inserted by the book-keeper, to whom I have already allowed a few lines in I. ii. and II. i, I am not inclined to resist him. Whether the book-keeper thought it worth while to call upon Chapman or any one else for assistance, I do not know.

194–267 (*Caliban and Mariners*).
The mixture of prose and verse is analogous to that in II. ii. and III. ii.

There are five broken lines (207, 219, 234, 250, 267), all speech-endings.

Act V, Scene 1 (*Reconciliation*)

(*a*) Mr. Wilson notes ten broken lines, 'some of which may have arisen from revision'. Of these eight (57, 87, 101, 103, 171, 173, 263, 281) are speech-endings, followed in one case (57) by music, in another (87) by a song, and in a third (171) by a discovery; one (299) is an extra-metrical interruption.

The tenth is more abrupt, but explicable by a change of addressee.

> A solemn air and the best comforter
> To an unsettled fancy cure thy brains,
> Now useless boil within thy skull: there stand,
> (61)   For you are spell-stopped.
> Holy Gonzalo, honourable man.

An eleventh, not noted by Mr. Wilson, is filled by a pause of surprise.

> Pros.   for I
> (148)   Have lost my daughter.
> Alonso   A daughter?

A twelfth (278), also not noted, is another extra-metrical interruption.

(*b*) There is one misdivision, for which any reason, other than a misprint, is hard to find.

> (95)   Why, that's my dainty Ariel: I shall miss
> Thee, but yet thou shalt have freedom: so, so, so.

(*c*) Mr. Wilson says, 'The extra-metrical and detached "No" given to Prospero at l. 130 is curious and can best be explained by a "cut" in the text, which deprives us of the rest of the retort.' It is not, however, unmetrical.

Pro.   I will tell | no tales. |
Seb.   The devil | speaks in | him.
Pro.   No!

(*d*) Prospero says (248):

                      at pickt leisure
    (Which shall be shortly single) I'le resolue you,
    (Which to you shall seem probable) of euery
    These happen'd accidents.

It is a characteristic involution in Shakespeare's latest manner, but hardly justifies Mr. Wilson's inference that 'the extreme awkwardness suggests adaptation'.

Finally, Mr. Wilson notes that 'this is the only occasion, apparently, in the whole canon where speakers who have concluded one scene appear again at the opening of the next. It is practically certain that some intervening scene has been deleted between iv. i. and v. i.' Dr. Greg has already called attention to the analogy of *M.N.D.* iii–iv, where Hermia and Helena 'sleepe all the Act'. In any case I doubt whether Shakespeare had any conscious practice in the matter.

Summary

The 'problem', if there is a 'problem', of *The Tempest* resolves itself into three issues.

1. Is there any reason for attributing the verse of the mask to another hand than Shakespeare's?

2. Is there sufficient evidence, 'bibliographical' or literary, for inferring abridgement, either to make room for the mask or for any other purpose?

3. Is there any such evidence for one or more recasts of the play as a whole?

To all three questions I give substantially negative answers. As to the first I have nothing to add to my notes on iv. i. Abridgement is claimed on five grounds: (*a*) the shortness of the play, (*b*) mute or semi-mute personages, (*c*) broken lines, (*d*) misdivision of lines, (*e*) incoherencies and obscurities.

a) *Shortness.* The play is short, and no doubt a short text is sometimes, as probably in *Macbeth*, due to abridgement. Some might argue that *The Tempest* is short because it was written for a court performance, but I have no reason for supposing that court performances were normally shorter than public performances. I would suggest, however, that in this case the length of the actual performance was sensibly increased by the songs and dumb-show episodes, of which several (iii. iii. 20, 53, 83; iv. i. 138, 193, 256; v. i. 57) give opportunity for elaborate treatment.

(*b*) *Mutes and Semi-mutes.* I have referred above to the sketchy treatment of Francisco, who however is required to make up an attendant for each of the principal nobles; Alonso, who has Gonzalo; Sebastian, who has Adrian, and Anthonio. Mr. Wilson also lays stress upon the fact that no more is heard in the play of a 'brave son' of Anthonio, whom Ferdinand (i. ii. 438) saw in the wreck, and thinks him a survival from an earlier version. But I doubt whether such a dropped thread is beyond Shakespeare's carelessness.

(*c*) *Broken Lines.* There are forty in all. Of these twenty-eight are speech-endings, followed in fourteen cases by an entry, or discovery, or episode of mask or music, or peal of thunder, or by a transition to prose or trochaics. This is a normal phenomenon of Shakespeare's later work, in which the tendency to depart from the tyranny of the line-unit leads to medial speech-endings, with the incidental result that an interruption sometimes leaves these in suspense. Six are self-contained exclamations or interjections, one (i. ii. 159) being of the 'amphibious' type which serves as end to one full line and beginning to another. These also are normal. One (v. i. 148) is divided between two speakers, and filled out by a pause of astonishment. There remain five which come in mid-speech. Two (i. ii. 316; v. i. 61) are explained by a change of addressee, or alternatively in the first case by a book-keeper's insertion; one (i. ii. 195) by a pause for consideration. Only two (i. ii. 235, 253) suggest to me possible cuts, and these probably, from the context, only of small extent. The position is very different from that in *Macbeth*, with its numerous, abrupt, mid-speech, broken lines, which are, I think, evidence of substantial abridgement.

(*d*) *Misdivisions.* Blank verse lines are often wrongly divided, both by Quarto and Folio printers, and the confusion sometimes extends over a series of successive lines. In these cases there is plausibility in Mr. Wilson's explanation that a compositor might be misled by a blank verse insertion, written continuously in a margin of manuscript too narrow to allow each line to be set out at full length. Of course, a marginal insertion is not necessarily evidence of abridgement, still less of wholesale recast. It may be evidence of expansion. On the other

and, its purpose may be to join the edges of a cut. The misdivisions in *The Tempest*, however, are not, except in one case,
of the serial type, and they are really very few in number,
compared with those in several other Folio texts. Mr. Wilson
(p. 79) says that they 'abound', but, apart from the confusion
between prose and verse in certain scenes, he only notes nine
examples. Of these four (i. ii. 309; ii. i. 244; iii. iii. 13; iv. i.
266) are merely space saving, generally by setting a speech
which ends one metrical line and begins another as one print-
line instead of two. One (i. ii. 361) is, I think, the sequel of a
misprint. One (v. i. 95) is perhaps itself a misprint. Two, one
of which is serial (ii. i. 192, 195–8), may result from some
trivial alteration; and one, involving two separate lines (i. ii.
301, 304), is, I think, possibly part of an insertion by the
book-keeper. There is nothing here to support a theory of
systematic abridgement.

e) *Incoherencies and Obscurities.* I have dealt with, and dis-
missed as trivial, in view of Shakespeare's occasional carelessness, the inconsistent replies of Miranda and the rambling pre-
history of Sycorax and Caliban, both in i. ii. Nor can I attach
much importance, pending a personal study of the Locatelli
scenari, to the converging attempts of Mr. Gray and Mr. Wilson to show that some episode or episodes may have dropped
out from iv. On the other hand, I think that the desire of the
producer to bring in Ariel as a nymph of the sea in i. ii. and to
give him a song in ii. i. may have led the book-keeper to introduce a slight confusion into each of these scenes.

So much for abridgement. I come now to the question of
recasts. And here I find it a little difficult to follow Mr. Wilson's theory, although I must remember that he does not profess to give a complete account of the fortunes of *The Tempest*
copy. At one place (p. 79) he writes as if he regarded the mixture of prose and verse in certain scenes, and also the length
of i. ii, as being further evidence of abridgement. I do not see
how they can be that; and in fact, when he comes to deal with
the 'mixed' scenes in detail, his suggestion is clearly that these
were verse-scenes 'in the original unrevised play' and that 'the
prose or part-prose sections probably represent pages of the
MS. which have undergone revision'. I understand him to
trace two distinct recasts. The first was when 'late in his
career' Shakespeare took up 'an old manuscript, possibly an
early play of his own', which was at any rate partly in rhyme,

and revised it by getting rid of the rhyme and turning some verse passages into prose. This still left *The Tempest* 'a loosely constructed drama, like *A Winter's Tale* and *Pericles*', in which Prospero's deposition, the birth of Caliban, and Claribel's voyage to Africa furnished material for pre-wreck scenes. I am assuming that Mr. Wilson would not cite *A Winter's Tale* and *Pericles* as analogies for the form of an early play by Shake-speare, and, if so, it must have been at a second recast that he supposes the pre-wreck scenes to have been omitted and re-placed by the three expositions. I am not quite clear whether any part of the general abridgement is supposed to have taken place at this stage, or whether that formed a third stage. Per-haps Mr. Wilson is not quite clear either. In any case, the mask was introduced 'when the play had already taken final shape under Shakespeare's hand'; and that apparently involved further abridgement. I am, however, now only concerned with the two general recasts. For the first the evidence is:

(*a*) The relation of the play to *Die Schöne Sidea*. Some com-mon source is, I think, probable; but it was not necessarily a play, and if a play, it was not necessarily in a relation of 'con-tinuous copy' to *The Tempest*.

(*b*) The 'traces of rhymed couplets'. I have noted above the four indicated by Mr. Wilson in III. i. and III. iii. He says that others occur 'elsewhere'. Perhaps he has in mind

I. ii. 304   And hither come in't: go: hence
             With diligence.

But this is probably the book-keeper. There is also

IV. i. 123   So rare a wonder'd father and a wise
             Makes this place Paradise.

Here some copies of the Folio read 'wife', which Mr. Wilson may be right in regarding as an emendation. But I suppose that in Mr. Wilson's view the lines would have been an inser-tion with the mask. There may be others. But such accidental rhymes, whether final or internal, seem to me due to Shake-speare's carelessness or whim, and no evidence of revision.

(*c*) Three lines of doggerel (III. ii. 86–8) in the mouth of Trinculo are, surely, too slight a basis for any argument, al-though I do not think there is any other doggerel in the plays later than *Lear*, I. v. 55–6.

(*d*) The 'mixed' passages. If Mr. Wilson's theory that these are due to partial revision of an 'early' play were correct, I should expect to find the verse sections in 'early' verse, and possibly in rhymed verse. But it is not so. The verse is all of a piece with that in the rest of the play, and distinctly late in manner, and if the verse, as well as the prose, belongs to the revision, then the reason for the differentiation is still to seek. To me it presents no great difficulty. There are other examples in which Shakespeare seems to have thought a variation of medium appropriate to transitions between more and less exalted subject-matter within the same scenes.

There is nothing to bear out this supposed second recast except the length of I. ii. and the three expositions, here and in II. i. Most of the second scene 'is taken up with an account of events which we may assume provided material for pre-wreck scenes in the earlier version'. It is indeed an assumption. But 'the expositions are there, and they tell their own tale'. I think they do. They tell that Shakespeare, having a great deal of pre-history to narrate, found it less tedious to do it at thrice than at once. But I do not see how they tell Mr. Wilson's. Shakespeare, at the end of his career, took it into his head to vary the loose construction of such plays as *A Winter's Tale* and *Pericles* by a final experiment on the lines of temporal unity. He reverted to the method of preliminary exposition which he had employed long ago for a similar theme in the *Comedy of Errors*. Why should we 'assume' that he put himself to the superfluous trouble of first writing *The Tempest* as a loose romance, and then converting it to unity? The break with his immediate past would have been no less deliberate.

1925.

THE STAGE OF THE GLOBE

In order to obtain a full understanding of any distinct mode o artistic expression, it is necessary to track it to its source, an to study the conditions under which its original utterance were shaped and its character and conventions took their ever lasting bent. Thus romance first becomes intelligible when you have learnt the life-history of the minstrel folk who gave i birth; and the refrains and rhythms of lyric yield a new mean ing, as you discern in them the uplifting of choric feet abou the sacred tree, or the swaying bodies of the oarsmen at th rowlock or the women at the loom. Above all is this true in th case of forms so elaborate as those of drama, whose very exis tence depends upon the substitution of costly co-operation fo the freedom of the single-handed entertainer, and whose tradi tions early attain to a stability based upon the conservatism o a syndicate and the permanence of an architectural structure If then one desires to differentiate the drama of the Renaissanc from the drama of the Middle Ages on the one side, or th drama of the Restoration on the other, it is almost inevitable t begin by determining the nature of the stage upon which th Renaissance plays were produced, and estimating the reactio which its dimensions and arrangement must have had upon th putting-together and the presentation of these.

Such an investigation is congenial enough to a generatio whose historic sense has been rendered acute by contact wit the pregnant conceptions of evolutionary science and philoso phy. More than one attempt has been made in recent years t reconstruct a Shakespearean stage and to remodel histrioni methods, perverted by the misunderstandings of two centuries in harmony therewith. As in all matters concerning Shake speare, German enterprise has taken a foremost and honourabl share in this endeavour. As far back as 1840 Karl Immerman produced *Twelfth Night* upon a stage designed by himself fo the purpose at Düsseldorf. Immermann's experiment was a isolated one, and he did not as a matter of fact arrive at any thing very closely approaching what we can imagine a Shake spearean stage to have been. It was not until 1888 that th discovery by Dr. Karl Theodor Gaedertz of a drawing of th interior of the Swan theatre, of which more will be said below stimulated a really widespread interest in the matter. The famous Munich Shakespeare-Bühne, organized by Karl von Perfall and Jócza Savits, was opened with a performance of *King Lear* on 1 June 1889, and yielded a long series of Shakespearean and other plays up to 1905. The example of Munich was followed more spasmodically at Breslau and Prague; and at Paris, in a production of *Measure for Measure* at the Théâtre de l'Œuvre in 1898. The English Elizabethan Stage Society, under the direction of Mr. William Poel, initiated its Shakespeare stage with a performance of *Measure for Measure* in 1893, and endured until 1905. In America the Department of English of Harvard University built an Elizabethan stage for a revival of Ben Jonson's *Epicœne* in 1895, and rebuilt it in accordance with the latest research for Mr. Forbes-Robertson to play *Hamlet* upon in 1904. It must of course be borne in mind that these ventures, with the possible exception of the Harvard one, were conceived in the interests of histrionic reform rather than in those of pure archaeology. The two objects are related, but ought not to be confused. The representation of Shakespeare's plays on the modern theatre has no doubt come to disaster, partly owing to the substitution after the Restoration of a picture-stage for a platform-stage, and partly owing to the bad taste of nineteenth-century stage-managers—notably Sir Henry Irving and Mr. Beerbohm Tree—who have persisted in elaborating scenic effect along lines of cost rather than of beauty, with results to the structure and movement of the plays no less ruinous than the havoc wrought by eighteenth-century adapters upon their texts. Obviously such reforms are required as will enable the dialogue of a play to be given in its entirety and in the order in which it was written; will prevent breaches of continuity in the progress of each act; and will restore declamation to its proper place in the equipment of the mime. I have seen nothing more ridiculous than a recent revival of *Richard II*, in which the performer of John of Gaunt, instead of coming forward to the footlights and spouting the patriotic harangue at the beginning of the second act, spoke it in the arms of his attendants, and with realistic representations of the feeble gestures, the halting utterance, and the broken accents of a dying man. Probably the actors themselves are more to blame than even the carpenters and the scene-shifters; but clearly if any kind of scenic illusion lends to the mutilation either of the words or of the spirit of a play as Shakespeare wrote it, that particular kind of scenic illusion stands self-condemned. On the other hand, it seems to me a mere pedantry to maintain that no scenic illusion can possibly be appropriate in the performance of Shakespeare's plays upon a modern stage, which was not available in the sixteenth century. The Elizabethan companies were limited by their poverty, by their mobility, and by the imperfect development of mechanical invention. It is difficult, in view of Shakespeare's apologies in the choruses to *Henry V* for his 'wooden O' and its 'unworthy scaffold', and for the

> Four or five most vile and ragged foils,
> Right ill-disposed in brawl ridiculous,

that must needs body forth the great name of Agincourt, to feel that he would not have gladly welcomed more spacious and decorative opportunities. And have not his lavish passages of description, such as that of Cleopatra's barge upon the Cydnus, again and again the effect of verbal scene-painting, making its appeal to the imagination through the ear in default of the eye? Probably the scenic reformer's best course is, while preserving the essentials of the Shakespearean theatre, so far as he can discover them, to allow himself to be guided in details by his own sense of beauty rather than by a minute respect for archaeology. After all, perhaps it comes to much the same thing in the long run. Mr. Gordon Craig hangs his stage with curtains, because they are more beautiful and mysterious than painted scenes, and in so doing he half unconsciously reproduces the folded arrases of the Globe.

To the scholar, on the other hand, the archaeological detail is important for its own sake and quite apart from any artistic use that may, by reproduction or adaptation, be made of it. The disinterested curiosity of his imagination will not be at rest until he knows precisely how it was all done at the time; and the very difficulty of the inquiry is his lure. This difficulty does not arise so much from any paucity of material, as from the failure of the material which exists to group itself into a coherent picture. The sources of information are, indeed, both varied and numerous. In the first rank are the few engravings and drawings which show the interior of a playhouse. Of these there are only four dating from before the end of the seventeenth century; and one of them, that of the Red Bull in 1672, is already too late to throw much light upon the Shakespearean

period. Two little wood-cuts are found upon the title-pages respectively of William Alabaster's *Roxana* (1632) and Nathaniel
Richards's *Messallina* (1640). These have received less attention than the drawing of the Swan already referred to, which is
a contemporary copy by one Arend van Buchell of Utrecht of
an original sketch made by his friend John de Witt during a
visit to London about 1596. Hardly less valuable than such
representations are the specifications for the building of the
Fortune in 1600 and of the Hope in 1613, which are contained
in builders' contracts and preserved amongst Alleyn's papers
at Dulwich. Much is to be gleaned from the innumerable allusions in controversial pamphlets concerning the stage, or in
literary works, such as the chapter on 'How a Gallant should
behave himself in a Playhouse' in Thomas Dekker's *The Gull's
Hornbook* (1609) and the prologues to several of Ben Jonson's
comedies. Finally there is the vast store of evidence furnished
by the stage-directions which are found to a greater or less
extent in nearly all the early printed editions of plays. Some of
these may have been added for the benefit of the reader in the
process of preparing a play for press; but the majority appear to
be genuine directions inserted by the author or the bookholder
into acting copies for the guidance of the actors and the tiremen; or, in the case of pirated editions, notes of the action made
from amongst the audience as it actually took place upon the
stage. They are full of indications illuminating, if indirect, of
the properties used, of the doors by which entrances and exits
were effected, and of the stage-devices of curtains and traverses
and arrases, of trap-doors and descending thrones, of scenes
'within' and scenes 'above', by which the plots were advanced
and changes of locality secured. It is unfortunate that, when
the material so gathered comes to be arranged and interrogated,
the inferences drawn from it prove singularly inconclusive and
conflicting. It has long been apparent that generalities about
the Elizabethan stage run a risk of being misleading. The
methods of presentation were probably more various than can
be comprehended in a single formula. Fundamental similari-
ties of principle must have been consistent with considerable
divergences on minor points, such as the number of the doors
or the position of the curtains. This is hardly surprising, when
one reflects on the wide diversity of experience which was available for the assistance of the early designers of stages. Doubtless the inn-yards in which the London companies had been

accustomed to play for over a quarter of a century formed their principal models; but in adapting these they could draw upon suggestions from many quarters, from miracle-play platforms of every shape and size with their *domi* and their *sedes*, from the pageants, movable and stationary, of processions and royal entries, from notions of the Roman theatre gathered by scholars from Vitruvius and the commentators upon Terence, from the makeshifts of guildhall and banqueting-house, and from the rings of scaffolding which accommodated the spectators at bear-baiting and at bull-baiting. Clearly the way in which plays were given at Court, when all the resources of the Revels Office, with its carpenters and its painters and its wire-drawers, were at the disposal of the company, must have differed much from the way in which they were furnished forth from the company's own stock of costumes and properties, before the city appren-tices and their lady-loves. Clearly also the arrangements and the manners of the so-called 'private' houses, such as the Black-friars, were not quite those of the great open public stages. And it is not always obvious for which type of performance the stage-directions of any particular print may have been intended. Even the great stages themselves may have been distinguished from each other by peculiarities of structure and contrivances which it is now impossible to recover. So that in the end the general inquiry as to the nature of the Shakespearean stage reduces itself to the more particular inquiry as to the nature of the stage of the Globe; and one's reliance upon the stage-directions, even of plays clearly traceable to the Chamberlain's or the King's company, can only be hesitating, when it is re-membered that some of the extant versions of these plays may have been specially prepared for Court, or for the provinces, that even during the latter years of Shakespeare's life the com-pany regularly performed at the Blackfriars as well as at the Globe, and that in its more unsettled early days it made its appearance, certainly or probably, upon the boards of Newing-ton Butts, the Rose, the Cross-Keys, the Theater, and the Curtain.

Certain misconceptions may at once be got rid of. Malone, by just such a critical misapplication of stage-directions not really referring to the public stage as is here deprecated, was led to assume the existence of a front curtain, which, however, he conceived, instead of being dropped like that now in use, to have opened in the middle and to have been drawn back-

wards and forwards on an iron rod. Hardly any one now, with
the exception of Mr. Sidney Lee, believes in this front curtain,
which indeed, in view of the relation of the stage to the auditorium, must, if it existed at all, have been accompanied by
similar curtains running along the sides of the stage from front
to back. But it did not exist. Such curtains as were used, were
hung, roughly speaking, at the back rather than at the front of
the stage and divided it from a room behind, which served as
the tiring-house of the actors. We learn that at the Fortune
the curtains were of worsted, and that it was the rude custom
of the audience to fling tiles and pears against them before the
beginning of the play, in order to allure the actors forth. Similarly it is clear that scenes, in the modern sense of cloths
painted in perspective, fastened upon rollers, and shifting to
indicate change of locality, although they were introduced from
Italy at the beginning of the seventeenth century and were used
in masques at court and in university plays, found no footing
upon the public stage until D'Avenant opened his house in
Lincoln's Inn Fields after the Restoration.

Some more positive notion of the structural character of the
Globe may be gleaned from the builder's contract for the Fortune, which has already been mentioned. In 1600 the Globe
was the latest new thing in theatres, and in entering into his
agreement for the Fortune with Peter Streete the carpenter,
Henslowe was careful to specify that the Globe should be taken
as the model, alike as regards the arrangement of the galleries
and staircases, the contrivance and fashioning of the stage, and
all other minor points not particularly set out. The only alterations of design asked for by Henslowe were that the scantlings
or standard measurements of the timber should be rather
stouter than those of the Globe, and that the main posts of the
stage and auditorium should be shaped square and carved with
figures of satyrs. It has been thought that the Globe was a
round theatre, but as the Fortune was certainly square, and as
Henslowe does not suggest any dissimilarity of shape, this must
be held doubtful. If it was square, the 'wooden O' of *Henry V*
must refer to some earlier theatre, probably the Curtain. In
view of Henslowe's allusions to the Globe, it is reasonable to
accept the features and the dimensions of the Fortune, as set
out in the specification, for a fair indication of the approximate
features and the dimensions of its rival. If so, the Globe was
eighty feet square without and fifty-five feet square within.

The framework was composed of three tiers, stories, or galleries of seats. These were respectively twelve, eleven, and nine feet high, and each of the upper ones jutted forwards ten inches in front of that beneath. The galleries were reached by staircases, and parts of them were divided off by partitions, so as to afford four gentlemen's rooms or boxes and a sufficient number of twopenny rooms. The stage was forty-three feet wide and projected forwards to the middle of the floor-space or yard. It had a tiring-house, and if this occupied a depth of twelve and a half feet, which would have been equal to that of the galleries, it would have left a depth of twenty-seven and a half feet for the stage. It will be seen that the stage was completely surrounded on three sides by the auditorium. Over the stage was a 'shadow or cover'. This, with the galleries and their staircases, was tiled and fitted with gutters to carry away rain-water backwards. The yard was evidently uncovered, and as the performances were in the afternoon, artificial lighting was thereby rendered unnecessary. The stage and the lowest story of the framework were paled in below, and the latter was also protected by iron pikes. The building was plastered outside; the rooms were ceiled; and the tiring-house was provided with glazed windows.

These data, valuable as they are, are not exhaustive. They leave us in the dark as to the position of the curtains, and as to the arrangements for entrances and exits and for changes of locality. Conjecture on these points has generally helped itself by transferring to the Globe some or all of the features disclosed in John de Witt's drawing of the Swan. This drawing in many respects confirms the indications of the Fortune contract. It shows the three tiers of seats and the stage surrounded by these and projecting into the middle of the yard. The general outline of the auditorium is round or oval instead of rectangular; and, perhaps in consequence of this, the width of the stage is not, as in the Fortune, markedly greater than its depth. In fact, after allowing for perspective, the proportions seem to be reversed. There are no palings round the stage, and two solid trestles which support it are visible. There is a 'shadow or cover', but this appears to be little more than a penthouse extending over the back of the stage and to be carried by two heavy round columns with square bases, planted in the floor of the stage about a third of the way from the back wall. I say 'appears', because, as will be seen, I have my doubts. The back wall itself is marked *mimorum aedes*, and in it are shown two pairs of large folding doors which doubtless give upon the tiring-house. Above these runs an open balcony divided into six boxes, in which persons are represented sitting. This is approximately on the level of the second gallery. The 'shadow' slopes down from the level of the third gallery, and above it towers a hut or cabin, with a door looking over the roof of the auditorium, at which stands a figure who seems to be blowing a trumpet. A flag with a swan upon it floats from the roof of the cabin. No curtain is apparent in any part of the stage.

The Fortune contract and the Swan drawing have been the starting-points for various efforts of imaginative reconstruction. The dominant theory may be taken to be that which is summed up and illustrated with a conjectural ground-plan and elevation in Dr. Cecil Brodmeier's *Die Shakespeare-Bühne nach den alten Bühnenanweisungen* (1904). It is also represented by the Harvard stage, as described and figured by Professor G. P. Baker in the German Shakespeare Society's *Jahrbuch* for 1905. According to this theory, the stage was divided into an inner and an outer part by a 'traverse' or curtain, moving to right and left on a rod, which was fixed between two columns placed as they appear to be shown by De Witt. The outer stage was used for the large number of scenes which take place in a garden or street or some other, often not very clearly defined, out-of-doors locality, and make very little, if any, demand for furniture or properties. The inner stage, for which the 'shadow' served as a roof, was hung at the back with arras, and was used for the representation of interiors. It is held that the continuous succession of scenes within each act of a play was rendered possible by the alternating use of these two spaces, since the inner stage was approached by doors from the tiring-house, and could be set and re-set with suitable properties, whilst action was proceeding on the outer stage in front of the traverse. Some of these outer scenes, in consequence, are of the nature of what a later theatrical jargon calls 'carpenters' scenes', serving rather to facilitate the process of alternation than notably to advance the plot. A still further variety of action was rendered possible by the gallery, which ran along the back wall of the inner stage above the arras. This formed a third or upper stage, and on it passed such scenes or parts of scenes, on the walls of cities, in Juliet's balcony, and the like, as are commonly indicated in stage-directions by the terms 'above' and 'aloft'. The traverse between the columns was high enough to shut out the upper stage, as well as the inner stage, from view; but the former also had its own short traverse, by means of which it could, if desired, be put out of action when the inner stage was in use.

The theory here expounded has had to face a good deal of criticism, particularly in some interesting articles on 'Some Principles of Elizabethan Staging', contributed by Mr. George F. Reynolds to *Modern Philology* for 1905. I cannot trace the controversy in detail. To me the theory appears, in the main, sound, both as regards the three divisions of the stage, and as regards the method of securing continuous action by the alternating use of these divisions. It is not necessary to assume that the management of the alternation was always perfect, or that other, and sometimes more primitive, devices for overcoming the awkwardness of incongruously juxtaposed scenes were not occasionally resorted to. 'You shal haue *Asia* of the one side, and *Affrick* of the other', writes Sidney in 1581, 'and so many other vnder-kingdoms, that the Player, when he commeth in, must euer begin with telling where he is: or els, the tale wil not be conceiued.' In Sidney's time the players helped themselves and their audiences by hanging up sign-boards over the entrances, in order to indicate the locality to which the speakers who used each entrance were supposed to belong; and it must not be taken for granted that, a quarter of a century later, the conservatism of the mimes had wholly learnt to dispense with this piece of *naïveté*. My own criticism of the Fortune-Swan-Globe reconstruction must be limited to a single but not, I think, an unimportant point. I do not see how the central traverse, between the inner and the outer stage, can possibly have come where Dr. Brodmeier and the Harvard architect put it. To this arrangement there are two principal objections. In the first place, how were entrances and exits effected when the traverse was closed and the outer stage alone in use? Dr. Brodmeier's plan only permits of them through the traverse itself. There were occasions when this would have been grotesque; as, for example, Act II, Scene iii, of *Cymbeline*. The inner stage represents Imogen's bedchamber in which the trunk scene has just taken place. On the outer stage Cloten is serenading Imogen. Cymbeline enters and says:

> Attend you here the door of our stern daughter?
> Will she not forth?

Obviously he cannot himself have just entered through that door.

I suppose that at Harvard such exits and entrances were managed round the edge of the stage beyond the columns, and through the side curtains of the inner stage. The grotesqueness would be avoided by this plan, since only a few of the audience would see the use made of the side curtains. But indeed the side curtains raise more difficulties than they solve; and this brings me to my second objection. The galleries in which the audience sat ran, as De Witt's drawing shows, right round the house until they came into contact with the back wall of the stage. If the traverse was closed and the tiremen were arranging beds and other properties upon the inner stage, the sides of the inner stage must have been closed also, or all the preparations would have been visible. This was recognized at Harvard, and supplementary traverses were provided, running back from the columns to the stage-wall. In Dr. Brodmeier's plan the sides of the inner stage are permanently closed, in order that he may obtain side entrances to the inner stage. But it does not seem to have been considered how this would affect the line of vision of the spectators at the stage ends of the auditorium. The depth from the columns to the back wall seems to be taken as from a third to a half of the whole depth of the stage, say from ten to fourteen feet. A fair number of Dr. Brodmeier's spectators would never see anything upon the inner or the upper stage, and would be seriously incommoded, when action was proceeding on the side of the outer stage farthest from them. The corresponding spectators at Harvard would be rather better off, because the side traverses would be drawn to give them a view of the inner scenes. But they also would often have their view of the outer stage blocked; and at the best surely these solid columns, with curtains clinging about them, must have proved very inconvenient obstacles to vision from various parts of the house, and must have provoked at least as much irritation and bad language as the largest *matinée* hat. My personal belief is that there were no columns and that therefore the traverse could not hang between them. I think of the Globe as a very simple affair, with a large open outer stage, forty-three feet wide by twenty-seven and a half deep, and a flat back wall hung with arras. Above is the balcony or upper stage with its short traverse; beneath the two doors to the extreme right and left, and between them another traverse, some thirty feet long, a parting in the middle of which furnishes the third door which some stage-directions imply. When this traverse is drawn, it discloses an inner stage contrived in the twelve and a half feet depth of the tiring-house and hung around with more arras. As this inner stage is what Mr. Reynolds calls an alcove, its traverse does not interfere with the use of the two principal doors or of the upper stage. It is not so large as the inner stage of the reconstruction already discussed, but surely quite large enough to represent a lobby, a study, a bed-chamber, a shop, a friar's cell, or the inside of a tomb. If a banqueting-hall or a court of justice was needed, it held the seats of state, and the rest of the action spread over the outer stage. Possibly it was raised two or three steps above the outer stage. It did not necessarily contain all the movable properties; such things as tables for a feast could easily be carried on to the outer stage, and carried away naturally enough when done with. The fact that all the action would be visible is really, I think, a great argument in favour of the simpler Globe.

And now, how did this notion of the forth-standing columns on the stage come about? The only possible evidence for them is that of the Swan drawing. I think it is just conceivable that De Witt did not regard them as supported on the stage at all, but as part of the structure of the back wall and set flush or nearly flush with the rest of this. If so, he drew them very badly. But then he drew the rest of his illustration very badly; and after all, he does not seem to have intended it as anything more than a rough note for the purpose of illustrating a certain analogy, which he fancied that he discovered between the structure of the Swan and that of the Roman *theatrum*. 'Cuius quidem formam', he says, 'quod Romani operis umbram videatur exprimere supra adpinxi.' It may even be doubted whether he did not do his drawing from memory after he got back to his inn. The trumpeter, for instance, would not really have been sounding when the action had already begun. Moreover, it is only Arend van Buchell's copy that we have, and not De Witt's original. Altogether the drawing cannot be insisted upon very much, as regards the exact position of the columns. This is especially so, in view of the fact that there are other grounds for thinking it highly improbable that there were any columns supported by this particular stage. In addition to the builder's contract for the Fortune in 1600, the Dulwich papers contain another made by Henslowe in 1613 with the carpenter

Gilbert Katherens for the building of the Hope. In this the model quoted in the specification is none other than the Swan. Katherens is to make the Hope 'of suche large compasse, fforme, widenes, and height' as is the Swan. The outside stair-cases are to be like those of the Swan, and the partitions be-tween the rooms are to be made as they are made at the Swan. The instructions as to the stage are noticeable. It is to be 'a stage to be carryed or taken awaie, and to stande vppon tressels good substanciall and sufficient for the carryinge and bearinge of suche a stage'. Similarly, Katherens must 'builde the Heavens all over the saide stage to be borne or carryed wthout any postes or supporters to be fixed or sett vppon the saide stage'. The 'heavens' are, of course, the same as the 'shadow or cover' of the Fortune. The reason for these arrangements at the Hope was that the building was to serve for bull-baiting and bear-baiting as well as for plays, and that for these purposes a permanent stage would be in the way. I have no proof that the Swan was used for baiting, although it was certainly used for acrobats, fencers, and spectacular entertainments; and it is possible that the movable stage and the heavens supported from above may have been features of the Hope, which were not copied from the Swan. But on the whole I think that the pre-sumption is the other way, particularly as the Swan stage is not paled in and its trestles are conspicuous in De Witt's draw-ing. Obviously, if the stage was movable, it could not support De Witt's columns. The Hope also was to have 'turned cul-lumes uppon and over the stage', and I believe that in both theatres these columns formed part of the decoration of the stage-wall. If they did not stand forward on the stage at the Swan, the reason, sufficiently flimsy beforehand, for putting them in that position at the Globe disappears altogether. They were not needed for support of the heavens, as the analogy of the Hope shows; and if these, at the Globe, were supported from the stage at all, the most convenient method would have been by comparatively slender posts rising from its outermost corners. I am assuming that the heavens of the Globe and the Fortune, like that of the Hope, covered the whole stage, and were not a mere penthouse such as is shown in the Swan draw-ing. Here again I believe that De Witt misrepresents the Swan, and that the heavens projected farther and sloped down much less than he indicates. Were it otherwise, they would obstruct the view from part of the topmost gallery; and it really must be assumed that even an Elizabethan architect meant the spectators to see something. Dr. Brodmeier's plan fails to guard against this obstruction. In the Harvard theatre the top gallery is well below the heavens, but these do not extend over more than the inner stage.

Many minor questions in connexion with the structure of the Globe call for solution. Were stools allowed for spectators upon the stage, and if so where were they placed? Where was the trap through which spirits arose and vanished? Was the balcony used solely as an upper stage, or did it also contain a music-room, and possibly the 'lords' rooms' or private boxes? And if the music-room and the lords' rooms were not there, where were they? What was the nature of the 'top' or 'tower' above the balcony, and how was the 'creaking throne' with its *deus ex machina* brought down from the heavens to please the groundlings? These are alluring themes, but within the limits of this paper it has seemed best to keep to fundamentals.

1907.

THE ORDER OF THE SONNETS

ANTIQUITY has left us little to go upon, as regards the origin and interpretation of Shakespeare's *Sonnets*, beyond the bare text of 1609. This was published by Thomas Thorpe, who prefixed his well-known dedication, 'To the onlie begetter of these insving Sonnets, Mr. W. H.'. In 1598, Francis Meres, in his *Palladis Tamia*, had referred to Shakespeare's 'sugred Sonnets among his priuate friends', and written of him as one of those 'most passionate among us to bewaile and bemoane the perplexities of Loue'. Two of the extant sonnets (CXXXVIII, CXLIV) had appeared in the miscellaneous collection of *The Passionate Pilgrime* (1599), boldly ascribed to Shakespeare, as a whole, by William Jaggard. On 3 January 1600 Eleazar Edgar registered 'a booke called Amours by J. D. with certen oy^r sonnetes by W. S.'. It is not extant, and we cannot say with any assurance who J. D. and W. S. were. In about 1613–16, William Drummond of Hawthornden, jotting down some notes on authors who had dealt with the subject of love, wound them up with 'The last we have are Sir William Alexander and Shakespear, who have lately published their Works'. The 'lately' might perhaps be held to point to the *Sonnets*, rather than to any earlier poems which had appeared under Shakespeare's name, but we do not know what information Drummond in Scotland is likely to have had as to the circumstances of their publication. Finally John Benson, issuing a very disorderly collection of Shakespeare's *Poems* in 1640, for which he certainly used the text of 1609, although without any fidelity, wrote of the contents of his volume that they 'in themselves appear of the same purity, the Authour himselfe then living avouched'. This may or may not refer to the *Sonnets* in particular, but it is at least possible that Benson knew of some statement by Shakespeare, which has not come down to us.

I discuss, in a separate essay, the possible identity of the youth, to whom the first series of sonnets (I–CXXVI) was addressed, with William, Lord Herbert, afterwards Earl of Pembroke, and also the date-range of that series, which I take to have been from the autumn of 1595 to that of 1599, or possibly a little later. There I, of course, take the edition of 1609 at its face value. But something must be said of the recurrent theory that the sonnets, as there printed, do not follow the order in which Shakespeare placed them, and that, by the exercise of critical ingenuity, an 'original order' can be recovered. The earlier attempts on these lines are, I think, negligible. At any rate, I will only deal here with the latest, which emerges from the careful research of Sir Denys Bray, and has received some measure of critical acceptance. Bray's *The Original Order of Shakespeare's Sonnets* (1925) was followed by a paper on 'The Art-Form of the Elizabethan Sonnet Sequence and Shakespeare's Sonnets' in the *Shakespeare-Jahrbuch* for 1927, and this again by *Shakespeare's Sonnet-Sequence* (1938), which repeats the arrangement of 1925, with some minor modifications.

One of the best editors of the *Sonnets*, Dr. H. C. Beeching, has grouped the first series of them, as they appear in Thorpe's text, under the following headings:

'The friend's beauty deserves immortality in children and in verse' (I–XIX); 'The poet's love for his friend' (XX–XXV); 'Thoughts in absence' (XXVI–XXXII); 'The friend's wrong-doing, confession, and forgiveness' (XXXIII–XXXV); 'The poet's guilt and the friend's truth; written in absence' (XXXVI–XXXIX); 'The friend's wrong to friendship' (XL–XLII); 'Thoughts in absence' (XLIII–LII); 'The friend's beauty and truth, which the poet will immortalize' (LIII–LV); 'The friend absents himself: the poet submits' (LVI–LVIII); 'Time and Beauty' (LIX, LX); 'The friend still absent' (LXI–LXV); 'The good old times' (LXVI–LXVIII); 'The friend's beauty and the world' (LXIX–LXX); 'The poet's death' (LXXI–LXXIV); 'The poet a miser' (LXXV); 'The poet's one theme' (LXXVI); 'With an album' (LXXVII); 'The poet has rivals, and one especially' (LXXVIII–LXXXVI); 'The poet appeals against the friend's estrangement' (LXXXVII–XCI); 'He dreads his unfaithfulness' (XCII–XCIII); 'Beauty and Vice' (XCIV–XCVI); 'Absence in summer and spring' (XCVII–XCIX); 'Apology for silence' (C–CIII); 'The friend's beauty and the poet's love, which are the argument of his verse, remain unchanged' (CIV–CVIII); 'Apology for apparent unfaithfulness during the long separation' (CIV–CXXV); 'Envoy' (CXXVI).

With the second series, which Bray keeps practically distinct from the first, I shall not concern myself. It has been, not inappropriately, described by Dr. J. W. Mackail, as 'a miscellaneous and disorderly appendix'.

Beeching's headings may be open to criticism in detail, but at least they serve to give a general map of the ground covered by the sonnets. I think that they are sometimes too comprehensive, and rather tend, by the wideness of their scope, to over-emphasize the element of grouping. There are many isolated sonnets, besides those for which they make allowance, which are best regarded as separate missives to, or perhaps only meditations on, the youthful friend. 'Absence' would, I think, be a normal condition of the relationship, although in some cases (XXVII–XXVIII, XLIV–XLV, XLVIII, L–LI) there is a definite reference to travel, which may suggest composition by Shakespeare during professional journeys, when communication, even by a post or other messenger, might be difficult.

On the other hand, many contiguous sonnets were clearly written, if not at one time, at any rate under a common impulse, and fall naturally into pairs or triplets or even larger groups. They may be linked in various ways. Sometimes there is a definite grammatical connexion, with the help of a 'Then', a 'Thus', a 'But', a 'Since', a 'So', an 'Or', through which argument flows on. Sometimes it is merely a matter of a continuous theme, as in the seventeen sonnets (I–XVII), which exhort the youthful friend to marry and beget children, or in the nine (LXXVIII–LXXXVI), which complain that he has found another poet. Often, however, the sense-linking of a group is emphasized by a definite stylistic device, which perhaps appealed more to Elizabethan than it does to modern literary taste. I have in mind the constant repetition of significant words and also, although less notably, that of rhyme-sounds, in sonnets so related. Thus the word 'beauty' is to be found in practically all of the opening group of encouragement to wedlock, and indeed 'beauty', 'love', and 'Time' run through the series as a whole. But in later groups the method, as applied to pairs or triplets of sonnets, presumably due to a single inspiration, becomes more elaborate. Here some examples will be of advantage. I italicize the linking elements.

XXVII

Weary with *toil*, I haste me to my bed,
The dear repose for limbs with travel tired;
But then begins a journey in my head,
To work my mind, when body's work's expir'd:
For then my thoughts—from *far* where I abide—
Intend a zealous pilgrimage to *thee*,
And keep my drooping eyelids open wide,
Looking on darkness which the blind do *see*:
Save that my soul's imaginary *sight*
Presents thy shadow to my sightless view,
Which, like a jewel hung in ghastly *night*,
Makes black *night* beauteous and her old face new.

Lo! thus, by *day* my limbs, by *night* my mind,
For *thee* and for myself no quiet find.

XXVIII

How can I then return in happy *plight*,
That am debarr'd the benefit of rest?
When *day's* oppression is not eas'd by *night*,
But *day* by *night* and *night* by *day* oppress'd,
And each, though enemies to either's reign,
Do in consent shake hands to torture *me*,
The one by *toil*, the other to complain
How *far* I *toil*, still *farther* off from *thee*.
I tell the *day*, to please him thou art *bright*,
And dost him grace when clouds do blot the heaven:
So flatter I the swart-complexion'd *night*;
When sparkling stars twire not thou gild'st the even.
    But *day* doth *daily* draw my sorrows longer,
    And *night* doth *nightly* make grief's strength seem stronger.

Take these, again.

XLIII

When most I wink, then do mine eyes best *see*,
For all the day they view things unrespected;
But when I sleep, in dreams they look on *thee*,
And darkly bright, are bright in dark directed.
Then thou, whose shadow shadows doth make bright,
How would thy shadow's form form happy *show*
To the clear day with thy much clearer light,
When to unseeing eyes thy shade shines *so*!
How would, I say, mine eyes be blessed made
By looking on *thee* in the living *day*,
When in dead night thy fair imperfect shade
Through heavy sleep on sightless eyes doth *stay*!
    All days are nights to see till I see *thee*,
    And nights bright days when dreams do show *thee me*.

XLIV

If the dull substance of my flesh were *thought*,
Injurious distance should not stop my *way*;
For then, despite of space, I would be brought,
From limits far remote, where thou dost *stay*.
No matter then although my foot did stand
Upon the furthest earth remov'd from *thee*;
For nimble *thought* can jump both sea and land,
As soon as think the place where he would *be*.

But, ah! *thought* kills me that I am not *thought*,
To leap large lengths of miles when thou art *gone*,
But that, so much of earth and water wrought,
I must attend time's leisure with my *moan*;
   Receiving nought by *elements* so *slow*
   But heavy tears, badges of either's *woe*.

XLV

The other two, slight air and purging fire,
Are both with *thee*, wherever I abide;
The first my *thought*, the other my desire,-
These present absent with swift motion slide.
For when these quicker *elements* are *gone*
In tender embassy of love to *thee*,
My life, being made of four, with two *alone*
Sinks down to death, oppress'd with *melancholy*;
Until life's composition be recur'd
By those sweet messengers return'd from *thee*,
Who even but now come back again, assur'd
Of thy fair health, recounting it to *me*:
   This told, I joy; but then no longer glad,
   I send them back again, and straight grow sad.

Or these:

LVII

Being your *slave*, what should I do but tend
Upon the *hours* and *times* of your desire?
I have no precious *time* at all to spend,
Nor services to do, till you require.
Nor dare I chide the world-without-end *hour*
Whilst I, my sovereign, watch the clock for you,
Nor think the bitterness of *absence* sour
When you have bid your servant once adieu;
Nor dare I question with my jealous thought
Where you may be, or your affairs suppose,
But, like a sad *slave*, *stay* and think of nought,
Save, where you are, how happy you make those.
   So true a fool is love that in your will,
   Though you do anything, he thinks no *ill*.

LVIII

That god forbid that made me first your *slave*,
I should in thought control your *times* of pleasure,
Or at your hand the account of *hours* to crave,
Being your vassal, bound to *stay* your leisure!

O! let me suffer, being at your beck,
The imprison'd *absence* of your liberty;
And patience, tame to sufferance, bide each check,
Without accusing you of injury.
Be where you list, your charter is so strong
That you yourself may privilege your *time*,
To what you will; to you it doth belong
Yourself to pardon of self-doing crime.
　　I am to wait, though waiting so be hell,
　　Not blame your pleasure, be it *ill* or well.

Or these:

LXIII

Against my *love* shall be, as I am now,
With *Time's* injurious *hand* crush'd and o'erworn;
When hours have drain'd his blood and fill'd his brow
With lines and wrinkles; when his youthful morn
Hath travell'd on to *age's* steepy *night*;
And all those *beauties* whereof now he's king
Are vanishing or vanish'd out of *sight*,
Stealing *away* the treasure of his spring;
For such a *time* do I now fortify
Against confounding *age's* cruel knife,
That he shall never cut from memory
My sweet *love's beauty*, though my *lover's* life:
　　His *beauty* shall in these *black* lines be seen,
　　And they shall live, and he in them still green.

LXIV

When I have seen by *Time's* fell *hand* defac'd
The rich-proud cost of outworn buried *age*;
When sometime lofty towers I see down-raz'd,
And *brass* eternal slave to *mortal* rage;
When I have seen the hungry ocean gain
Advantage on the kingdom of the shore,
And the firm soil win of the watery main,
Increasing store with loss, and loss with store;
When I have seen such interchange of state,
Or state itself confounded to *decay*;
Ruin hath taught me thus to ruminate—
That *Time* will come and take my *love away*,
　　This thought is as a death, which cannot choose
　　But weep to have that which it fears to lose.

LXV

Since *brass*, nor stone, nor earth, nor boundless sea,
But sad *mortality* o'ersways their power,
How with this rage shall *beauty* hold a plea,
Whose action is no stronger than a flower?
O! how shall summer's honey breath hold out
Against the wrackful siege of battering *days*,
When rocks impregnable are not so stout,
Nor gates of steel so strong, but *Time decays?*
O fearful meditation! where, alack,
Shall *Time's* best jewel from *Time's* chest lie hid?
Or what strong *hand* can hold his swift foot back?
Or who his spoil of *beauty* can forbid?
    O! none, unless this miracle have *might*,
    That in *black* ink my *love* may still shine *bright*.

Or these:

XCVII

How like a *winter* hath my *absence* been
From *thee*, the pleasure of the fleeting year!
What freezings have I felt, what dark days seen!
What old December's bareness every where!
And yet this time remov'd was *summer's* time;
The teeming autumn, big with rich increase,
Bearing the wanton burden of the prime,
Like widowed wombs after their lords' decease;
Yet this abundant issue seem'd to *me*
But hope of orphans and unfather'd fruit;
For *summer* and his pleasures wait on *thee*,
And, thou *away*, the very *birds* are mute;
    Or, if they sing, 'tis with so dull a cheer,
    That leaves look pale, dreading the *winter's* near,

XCVIII

From you I have been *absent* in the spring
When proud-pied April, dress'd in all his trim,
Hath put a spirit of youth in every thing,
That heavy Saturn laugh'd and leap'd with him.
Yet nor the lays of *birds*, nor the *sweet smell*
Of different *flowers* in odour and in hue,
Could make me any *summer's* story *tell*,
Or from their proud lap pluck them where they grew;

Nor did I wonder at the *lily's white*,
Nor praise the deep vermilion in the *rose*;
They were but *sweet*, but figures of delight,
Drawn after you, you pattern of all those.
   Yet seem'd it *winter* still, and, you *away*,
   As with your shadow I with these did play.

XCIX

The forward violet thus did I chide:
Sweet thief, whence didst thou steal thy *sweet* that *smells*,
If not from my love's breath? The purple pride
Which on thy soft cheek for complexion *dwells*
In my love's veins thou hast too grossly dy'd.
The *lily* I condemned for thy hand,
And buds of marjoram had stol'n thy hair;
The *roses* fearfully on thorns did stand,
One blushing shame, another *white* despair;
A third, nor red nor *white*, had stol'n of both,
And to his robbery had annex'd thy breath;
But for his theft, in pride of all his growth
A vengeful canker eat him up in death.
   More *flowers* I noted, yet I none could *see*
   But *sweet* or colour it had stol'n from *thee*.

I think that these examples are fairly typical of the clearly sense-linked groups. Of course a rhyme-word may be part of a word-link, as well as of a rhyme-link. I note that in XXVII–XXVIII there are five word-links and two rhyme-links; that in XLIII–XLV there are six word-links and four rhyme-links, one emphasized by repetition; that in LVII–LVIII there are six word-links and no rhyme-link; that in LXIII–LXV there are ten word-links and two rhyme-links, one imperfect; and that in XCVII–XCIX there are twelve word-links and two rhyme-links, one imperfect. In the friendship series, as a whole, I feel sure that the word-linking is the predominant factor. The words used to effect it are generally significant of the pervading emotional theme, whereas those in the rhyme-links are often not, except for the recurrent *me-thee*, which, in view of the general tenor of the series, was almost inevitable. I find no instance of a clearly sense-linked group which relies for its further linking upon rhyme alone. It should be added that some words used for links, such as *decay-decays* and *mortal-mortality* (LXIV–LXV) or *absent-absence* and *smell-smells* (XCVII–XCIX) are cognate, rather than identical; and also that there is sometimes much word-play within a sonnet, which does not aim at linking. A good example is XLIII, with its 'eyes' and 'bright' (each four times), 'sleep' (twice), 'dark', 'darkly', and 'shade', 'shadow', 'shadow's', 'shadows'.

I turn to Sir Denys Bray. Much as I differ from his conclusions, a salute is due to the ingenuity and thoroughness with which he has worked them out. He starts, as any critic must, from the evidence, already considered, that the sense-linking of sonnet-groups is often accompanied either by word-linking or by rhyme-linking, or by both. And this, as he rightly points out, is also a feature of other contemporary sonnet-sequences, such as those left us by Samuel Daniel, Edmund Spenser, Michael Drayton, Thomas Lodge, Thomas Watson, and lesser men. Some of these also use more formal linking devices, of which Shakespeare did not, as a rule, avail himself. Thus the last line or half-line of one sonnet may be repeated, perhaps in a slightly altered form, at the beginning of the next, and in Daniel, Spenser, and Drayton we can trace a yet subtler pattern, in which a run of rhyme-sounds throughout successive sonnets, at one point of a sequence, is echoed by a repetition of the same run later on. And now Bray is struck by a noble thought. In these others the use of rhyme-linking and word-linking was sporadic. But is it possible that Shakespeare resolved to go one better than his fellows, and to compose a sequence in which the linking should for once run in an unbroken chain from start to finish of a continuous poem? Obviously that is not so with the *Sonnets*, as they stand in the order of Thorpe's text. But is it possible that, for some reason or other, that text is a perversion? And can we, with the help of the clues which it affords, arrive at an 'original order', which does in fact represent Shakespeare's own intention? On these lines Bray sets to work, and does in fact arrive, by what he calls a 'jig-saw' process, through trial and error, at a sequence, in which the sonnets are attached to one another, both by a continuous succession of rhyme-links, and by an almost, although not quite, continuous succession of word-links. Perhaps one should rather say two sequences, since Bray still keeps apart the first and second series of sonnets, as we find them in Thorpe's text, although he provides a single rhyme-link between them. I need not go into the complication due to the possibility, that after originally writing his sequence with 'Thou' as the pronoun of address to his friend, Shakespeare later inserted other sonnets, in which he used 'You'. This problem, if it is one,

arises, even if we keep the order of Thorpe's text. Bray thinks
that the 'You' sonnets were afterthoughts, that Shakespeare,
before he wrote them, had kept the original cycle lying by him
long enough to pass unconsciously from one pronoun to the
other, but that, when inserting them, he was careful to provide
additional rhyme-links and word-links. My own impression is
that, writing at intervals, he used the two pronouns indif-
ferently. In any case, Dowden was wrong in supposing that to
the Elizabethans 'you' was the pronoun of intimate affection
and 'thou' that of respectful homage. A glance at the *Oxford
Dictionary* will show that the converse was the case.

Bray claims for his order that in it emerges, for the first time,
that device of rhyme-echoing between one group of sonnets and
another, which he found in other contemporary sequences.
Thus in a group, which he calls 'The Triumph of Love and
Beauty over Age and Time' (his 84–8, constructed from
Thorpe's c, LXIII, XIX, LXVIII, CIV), he finds an exact repetition
of words—'long', 'life-knife', 'pen-men', 'born', 'dead'—
which also occur, in the same order, in an earlier 'Forbodings of
Death' (his 42–6, similarly constructed from Thorpe's LXXIII,
LXXIV, LXXXI, LXVI, LXXI). There are other examples. And more
generally he argues that in his order for the first time, the sonnets answer to the Elizabethan conception of a sequence as an
elaborate art-whole, which has been obscured in that of Thorpe.

In the Quarto the rhymes lie in kaleidoscopic confusion. Throughout
the rhyme-linked, sense-linked reconstruction they have settled down into
a network of cyclical or rhythmical and typical Elizabethan pattern, only
explicable as the product of design.

A poet, he reminds us, like every other artist, is after all a
craftsman also, and Thorpe's order was wanting in 'continuity
or unity—the vital principle of art in all its forms'. It may be
so, but I am myself more inclined to look upon the unity of
Shakespeare's sonnets, written over three or more years, as an
autobiographical one, following the ups and downs of an emotional relationship, than as a planned attempt to develop a pre-
conceived dramatic design. It is fair to add that at one point
Thorpe's order seems to be open to the reproach of an inconsistency, which disappears in that of Bray. In Sonnets XXXIII–
XXXV Shakespeare reproves the youth for a wrong to friendship,
which involved a 'sensual fault', and from XL–XLII it is clear
that he had taken the poet's mistress. This is recalled, perhaps,
in CXX: 'That you were once unkind befriends me now'. In

xx, on the other hand, the youth is said to have been the mark
or 'slander'.

> For canker vice the sweetest buds doth love,
> And thou present'st a pure unstained prime.
> Thou hast pass'd by the ambush of young days,
> Either not assail'd, or victor being charg'd.

Perhaps the Elizabethan conception of a 'pure unstained
prime' was an easy-going one. Perhaps, on the other hand,
Shakespeare, at one point of the intercourse with his friend,
had wiped out the stain, in his charitable memory. In any case,
Bray escapes the apparent inconsistency by putting LXX (his 64)
earlier than XXXIII–XXXV (his 72, 73, 78).

I do not know how far the 'jig-saw' was a difficult process.
A normal sonnet may have seven rhyme-sounds and fourteen
rhyme-words. In the first series, as a whole, there are 1,076
rhyme-pairs. In the sequence, as a whole, the *-ee* sound occurs
about seventy times, the *-y* sound, which may link either with
the *-ee* sound or the *-ie* sound, about fifty times, the *-air*, *-art*,
-ie, *-ill*, *-o*, *-oan*, *-ue* sounds, over twenty times apiece. There
seems to be a good deal of room for permutations and combina-
tions here. I do not attach much importance to Bray's repeated
statements that particular words used in links are unique or
rare in 'Shakespeare's sonnet-vocabulary', with the implication
that they must have been deliberately chosen, in order to provide links. Shakespeare had all the Elizabethan vocabulary
there was to draw upon, and uses most of it in his plays. There
are in fact only about thirty words in the sonnets, which can
possibly be called recondite, and of these only half a dozen—
antique, canker, character, distill'd, invocate, wrack—are used as
links.

Bray has, of course, a crucial question to face. If his reconstruction is sound, how did it come about that the sonnets
appeared in a different order from their true one, when they
were printed in Thorpe's text? And indeed how did they reach
Thorpe's hands at all? Up to a point he has his answer ready,
although he admits that it is 'largely guess-work'. After the
development of Shakespeare's theme had led him into regions
of intimacy that made publication impossible, he still wrote on.

But in the end, perhaps soon after the last sonnet was penned, perhaps
years later, he broke the chain and disarranged the flowing whole, either
in artistic dissatisfaction with it, or, more probably, to ensure that what-

ever the future had in store, the heart that he had unlocked in his own inner chamber should not lie exposed for daws to peck at.

As to the daws, I am afraid that he has been disappointed. But why did he not destroy the sonnets outright? 'Surely', says Bray, 'beccause they were too glorious stuff for the writer to destroy.'

And so:

I for one find little difficulty in imagining that Shakespeare shrank from the publication of sonnets of such intimacy and shrank also from the destruction of such incomparable poetry, and simply put a disturbing hand into the flowing whole in which a storm-beaten chapter in his life lay revealed, in order to hide it from any prying or piratical Thorpe who came upon the Sonnets thereafter.

He did not, however, merge the first and second series into one. Two problems, I think, arise on this theory. How is it that, even in Thorpe's order, so much coherence is still to be found, that at least the outlines of the shifting relationship remain discernible? The shuffle must have been a very perfunctory one. Or were the sonnets, perhaps, sometimes written, not simply on separate sheets, but in pairs or triplets, which could not be divided? And again, how did the collection, even in its disorder, get out of Shakespeare's hands at all? Are we to fall back on Sonnet·XLVIII?

> How careful was I when I took my way,
> Each trifle under truest bars to thrust,
> That to my use it might unused stay
> From hands of falsehood, in sure wards of trust!

But, 'Thee have I not lock'd up in any chest'. Alternatively, did Thorpe get his copy, not from Shakespeare himself, but, as his dedication rather suggests, from the friend to whom the sonnets were written, and who may well not have been careful to preserve them in their proper order? We cannot say.

> Ah! What a dusty answer gets the soul
> When hot for certainties in this our life!

But my fundamental quarrel with Sir Denys really rests, not so much on what he has done, as on what he has undone. Intent upon his continuous chain of formal links, he has rent asunder many sense-links, sometimes even reinforced by grammatical conjunctions, which are clearly apparent in Thorpe's text. Examples may be found among the sonnets I have quoted

above. Thus xxvii and xxviii, closely linked by 'then' and by
the emphasis on *day* and *night* and *toil*, as well as by the rhymes,
become for him 38 and 41. So, too, the compact group on
Time (LXIII–LXV), with its 'Since' and its long series of word-
links, in *love, Time, hand, age, beauty, away, black, brass, mortal,
decay*, is split by Bray into his 85, 120, and 10. Consider again
the continuous word-play on the flowers in xcviii and xcix,
broken by his rearrangement of them as 82 and 89. But it will
be well, since this is a crucial point, to add yet other examples.
Take, then, xxx and xxxi (Bray's 116 and 4) on the loss of dead
friends.

XXX

When to the sessions of sweet silent thought
I summon up remembrance of things past,
I sigh the *lack* of many a thing I sought,
And with old woes new wail my dear time's waste;
Then can I drown an *eye*, unus'd to flow,
For precious *friends hid* in *death's* dateless night,
And weep afresh *love's* long since cancell'd woe,
And moan the expense of many a vanish'd sight:
Then can I grieve at grievances *foregone*,
And heavily from woe to woe tell o'er
The sad account of fore-bemoaned *moan*,
Which I new pay as if not paid before.
   But if the while I think on *thee*, dear *friend*,
   All losses are restor'd and sorrows end.

XXXI

Thy bosom is endeared with all hearts,
Which I by *lacking* have supposed *dead*;
And there reigns *Love*, and all *Love's loving* parts,
And all those *friends* which I thought buried.
How many a holy and obsequious tear
Hath dear religious *love* stol'n from mine *eye*,
As interest of the *dead*, which now appear
But things remov'd that *hidden* in *thee* lie!
Thou art the grave where buried *love* doth live,
Hung with the trophies of my *lovers gone*,
Who all their parts of me to *thee* did give,
That due of many now is thine *alone*:
   Their images I *lov'd* I view in *thee*,
   And thou—all they—hast all the all of me.

Or take LXVII and LXVIII, formally linked, once more by 'Thus', which are Bray's 62 and 87.

LXVII

Ah! wherefore with infection should he *live*,
And with his presence grace impiety,
That sin by him advantage should achieve,
And lace itself with his society?
Why should *false* painting imitate his *cheek*,
And steal dead seeing of his *living hue*?
Why should poor *beauty* indirectly seek
Roses of shadow, since his rose is *true*?
Why should he *live*, now *Nature* bankrupt is,
Beggar'd of blood to blush through *lively* veins?
For she hath no exchequer now but his,
And, proud of many, *lives* upon his gains.
    O! him she *stores*, to *show* what wealth she had
    In days long since, before these last so bad.

LXVIII

Thus is his *cheek* the map of days outworn,
When *beauty liv'd* and died as flowers do now,
Before these bastard signs of fair were born,
Or durst inhabit on a *living* brow;
Before the golden tresses of the dead,
The right of sepulchres, were shorn away,
To *live* a second *life* on second head;
Ere *beauty's* dead fleece made another gay:
In him those holy antique hours are seen,
Without all ornament, itself and *true*,
Making no summer of another's green,
Robbing no old to dress his *beauty new*;
    And him as for a map doth *Nature store*,
    To *show false* Art what *beauty* was of yore.

I could quote more examples, but these will suffice. Certainly, some of the sonnets concerned might stand well enough, individually, where Bray has placed them. But if they were written separately, I do not see how they can possibly have come to cohere, so closely as they do, with others in Thorpe's text, through the mere accident of a shuffle. And so I feel bound to reject, without hesitation, the whole of Bray's ingenious theory.

1943.

THE 'YOUTH' OF THE SONNETS

WRITING on the Sonnets in my *William Shakespeare* (1930), I came to the conclusion that, while there can be no certainty as to the identification of the youth to whom those in the longer series (I–CXXVI) were addressed, the most plausible theory was that which finds him in William, Lord Herbert, the son and heir of Henry, Earl of Pembroke, by his wife Mary, the sister of Sir Philip and Sir Robert Sidney. This view was mainly based on letters from Rowland Whyte, the London agent of Sir Robert, to his master at Flushing, which are now preserved at Penshurst Place in Kent. Extracts from these were printed by Arthur Collins in his *Letters and Memorials of State* (1746). And from them it became apparent that in the autumn of 1595 an attempt was made to betroth Herbert, born on 8 April 1580, and therefore no more than a boy of fifteen, to Elizabeth, daughter of Sir George Carey by his wife Elizabeth Spencer, and granddaughter of Henry Carey, Lord Hunsdon, then Lord Chamberlain of the Royal Household. The negotiation broke down, according to the letters printed by Collins, on financial grounds. But Collins did not give the full story, which was not revealed until Mr. C. L. Kingsford made further extracts from Whyte's letters, which were printed in the second volume of the *Report* on *The Penshurst MSS.* issued by the Historical Manuscripts Commission in 1934. It now became apparent for the first time that one factor in the collapse of the parental scheme was the reluctance of young Herbert to become engaged to the young lady, who was about four years his senior. Possibly she was not herself of a very coming-on disposition, since there had already been overtures in May 1595 for her marriage to Thomas, son of Henry, Lord Berkeley, whom in fact she married on 19 February 1596, and the family chronicler of the Berkeleys writes of affection already existing between them in the previous autumn (J. Smyth, *Lives of the Berkeleys*, ii. 383, 394–5). But it will be well to piece together the record of the Herbert-Carey affair from the extracts of Collins and Kingsford, neither of whom, taken alone, gives it quite in full. The ciphers were interpreted in the *H.M.C. Report*, ii. 643. All the letters are of 1595 (Collins, i. 353, 372; *Penshurst*, ii. 163, 173, 175, 177, 180, 182, 188, 194).

Sept. 25. My lady Carey and her daughter are gone to the Wight. Great preparacion was made for them at Wilton [Pembroke's house], but they came not their, I know not the occasion.

Oct. 8. My lord [of Pembroke] hymself, with my Lord Harbert [is] come vp to see the Queen, and (as I heare) to deale in the matter of a marriage with Sir George Careys daughter.

Oct. 15. As for my lady Careis not going to Wilton, I am informed that she expected at Court a dispatch in her sute for certain lands that shuld discend to her daughter, by being next of kinn unto her Majestie by the mothers syde; and lest the speach of marriage might overthrow it, 'twas thought best to put yt of till another tyme. My lord Harbart likewise being a suter for certain parkes and reversion, 'tis feared if the marriage were spoken of, that might bring hindrance unto yt. And therefore, here [London] is the place chosen fittest for the two young ones to have an enterview, where without suspicion they may ofte meete in secret, and to that end comes my lord of Pembroke up upon Monday next [Oct. 20]. I heare that yt is a motion very pleasing to both sydes; this is all that I can as yet learn.

Oct. 18. My lord of Pembroke's coming is put off, on a speech of the Lord Treasurer [Burghley] that it were good he lay at Milford Haven to strengthen those parts.

Oct. 25. My lord of Pembroke is here; so is my lord Harbert and both gonne to the Court.

Oct. 29. My lord of Pembroke and Lord Harbart are here; the Queen takes yt kindly that in this tyme of danger he came up to see her, and to offer hymself and fortune to doe her service. Their hath been an enterview between the parties, and as I heare 9000 [Herbert] wilbe hardly brought to affect *pp.qq* [Mistress Carey].

Nov. 5. 2000 [Pembroke] cannot get them to move 1500 [the Queen] for 9000 [Herbert] though he hath given them good cause.

Nov. 22. The speech of marriage between 9000 [Herbert] and *qq* [Elizabeth Carey] is broken off, by his not liking.

Dec. 5. Sir George Carey takes it very unkindly, that my Lord of Pembroke broke of the Match intended between my Lord Herbert and his Daughter, and told the Queen it was becawse he wold not assure him 1000^l. a year, which comes to his Daughter, as next a kinne to Queen Ann Bullen. He hath now concluded a marriage between his Daughter and my Lord Berkleys Sonne and Heire.

There can be no certainty, but clearly Herbert's 'not liking' brings us much nearer to the situation indicated by *Sonnets* I–XVII, than any other clue, which has yet been suggested. Of course, there is no mention of Shakespeare in Whyte's letters. But he had made a reputation for himself, as something more than a mere player, by his *Venus and Adonis* (1593) and his *Rape of Lucrece* (1594). And even as a player, he may well have

been a *persona grata* to Sir George Carey, the son of Lord Hunsdon, in whose company he was then a leading member, and to
the Earl of Pembroke, to whose company he had probably
belonged at an earlier date. If they wanted a plausible man to
stimulate the imagination of the young Herbert, they could
hardly have made a better choice.

Elizabeth Carey was not the only bride thought of in vain
for Herbert. In 1597 a match was suggested with Elizabeth
Vere, daughter of Edward, Earl of Oxford and granddaughter
of Lord Burghley. But this scheme also broke down. It is
Rowland Whyte, again, who records its stages (*Penshurst*, ii.
294, 297, 302, 305).

Oct. 8. I hear that 2000 [Pembroke] is resolved to accept the offer
made by 900 [Burghley], which is to give 3000^l, and assure 600^l a
year land after his decease.

Oct. 22. For the matter of 9000 [Herbert] it is upon a sudden quite
dashed, and in the opinion of the wise by great fault in 2000 [Pem-
broke], who makes the occasion of the breach to be a refusal of the por-
tion offered by 900 [Burghley]. 2000 [Pembroke] will have 3000^l in
money and 500^l a year in possession, else will he not bargain. 13 [un-
identified] grieves at it, for he foresees the harm will ensue.

Nov. 5. The matters of 9000 [Herbert] are quite broken off, and he
deceived you that said he was come to London.

Dec. 20. 9000 [Herbert] matters yesternight upon a soddain are like to
dye, for 9000 [error for 900, Burghley] thinkces that he is not well delt
withall by 2000 [Pembroke], who refused his offers, which are 3000^l in
money and 200^l a yeare in possessioon, and now wrytes to 2000 [Pem-
broke] that he will give no more till his death, and then 300^l a year
more, but 13 [unidentified] assures me yt will not be accepted.

There is, of course, no suggestion of Herbert's reluctance
here. In 1598 there was talk of a marriage with Elizabeth,
daughter of Sir Francis Gawdy and widow of Sir William
Hatton (T. Tyler, *Shakespeare's Sonnets*, 50), and in 1599 Rowland Whyte was trying to bring about one with a niece of
Charles Howard, Earl of Nottingham, mainly because Nottingham, as Lord Admiral, could advance Sir Robert Sidney's
affairs. But on 16 August 1600 he had to admit that he did
not 'find any disposition in this gallant young lord to marry'.
Ultimately, but not until 4 November 1604, Herbert did
marry Mary, daughter of Gilbert Talbot, Earl of Shrewsbury.
In the interval, he had seduced Mary Fitton, one of the Queen's
Maids of Honour, had been imprisoned for it, and had himself
become Earl of Pembroke at the death of his father on 19 Jan-

uary 1601. These things lie outside the ambit of the *Sonnets*.
Mary Fitton, known from her portrait at Arbury to have been
a fair beauty, cannot have been the black-eyed lady of the
second series of *Sonnets*, and indeed it is doubtful whether those
are linked with the first series at all. One could wish, however,
to have the letter described by William Cory as at Wilton in
1865, but no longer traceable there in 1898 (*W.S.* ii. 329).

The house (Lady Herbert said) is full of interest: above us is Wolsey's
room; we have a letter, never printed, from Lady Pembroke to her son,
telling him to bring James I from Salisbury to see *As You Like It*; 'we
have the man Shakespeare with us'. She wanted to cajole the King in
Raleigh's behalf—he came.

The apparent familiarity, with which Shakespeare seems to
have been referred to, is noteworthy, and there is in fact a
record of a payment to the King's Men for a performance at
Wilton on 2 December 1603.

A start for the first series in 1595 makes a reasonable
chronology possible. The image in Sonnet III,

> Thou art thy mother's glass, and she in thee
> Calls back the lovely April of her prime,

has its contemporary parallel of 1594 in *Lucrece* (ll. 1758–9),

> Poor broken glass, I often did behold
> In thy sweet semblance my old age new born.

We know from William Browne's lines and elsewhere that
Lady Pembroke was a beauty. So, too, those in XIV,

> But from thine eyes my knowledge I derive,
> And, constant stars, in them I read such art
> As truth and beauty shall together thrive,

may be compared with *Love's Labour's Lost* (1595), 'From
women's eyes this doctrine I derive' (IV. iii. 350).

One must not, of course, lay too much stress on verbal
parallels between the sonnets and the plays. Images, once in
the mind, tend to recur, even after long intervals. The reading
over of old work may perhaps sometimes refresh them. It is
most often in the plays of 1597 to 1601 that echoes from or to
the sonnets suggest themselves. But they run on even to the
Winter's Tale of 1611. In Sonnet CII we have 'As Philomel
in summer's front doth sing' and in *Winter's Tale* (IV. iv. 2)
'no shepherdess, but Flora, Peering in April's front'. Topical
allusions in the sonnets are not very common. The 'art made
tongue-tied by authority' of LXVI may refer to the restraint of

playing in July 1597. The 'pure unstained prime' ascribed to the youth in LXX must of course, if he was Herbert, antedate the Mary Fitton affair. The most likely equation for the rival poet of LXXVIII–LXXXVI is Samuel Daniel, who had been tutor to Herbert as a boy at Wilton, had dedicated to his mother his *Delia* (1593) and *Cleopatra* (1593), and was later to dedicate to Herbert himself his *Defence of Rhyme* (1603). An external reference to Shakespeare's 'sugred Sonnets among his priuate friends' first comes to us in the *Palladis Tamia* (1598) of Francis Meres. Two of them, but from the second series of 1609, not the first, are in *The Passionate Pilgrime* of 1599. The three years period of CIV, if it starts from the autumn of 1595, runs through the winters of 1595–6, 1596–7, 1597–8, and the springs and Junes of 1596, 1597, and 1598, to the autumn of 1598. The 'mortal moon' sonnet (CVII) I place in the next autumn, when the fear of a Spanish attempt had passed, and a prospect of peace seemed to be in sight. The 'thralled discontent' of CXXIV may have been that caused by the imprisonment at York House of the popular Earl of Essex, which lasted from 1 October 1599 to 5 July 1600, and led to the printing of slanderous libels and to seditious prayers and speeches by the Puritan clergy, some of which are referred to in Rowland Whyte's letters. On 3 January 1600 comes the entry in the *Stationers' Register* of 'Amours by J. D. with certen oy^r sonnetes by W. S.'. I should like to find John Donne and William Shakespeare linked. But initials are ambiguous and, if the book was ever printed, no copy of it is known. I do not find any evidence in the *Sonnets* themselves of a later date than 1599. As for Thomas Thorpe in 1609, I doubt whether he had anything before him but 'To W. H.' on a manuscript. Certainly, however, the Earl of Pembroke took no steps to suppress the publication, as he could easily have done, if he thought it worth while. The dedication of the *First Folio* plays to him and his brother in 1623 tells us that they had 'prosequuted both them, and their Author liuing, with so much fauour'. Pembroke became responsible for the supervision of Court entertainments when he was appointed as Lord Chamberlain in December 1615, but he had not much time to do favour in this capacity to Shakespeare before the poet's death on 23 April 1616.

1943.

THE 'MORTAL MOON' SONNET

THE date and significance of *Sonnet* CVII have evoked much controversy, determined in part by rival identifications of the 'youth' with the Earl of Southampton and with William, Lord Herbert. It will be well to give the text for easy reference.

> Not mine owne feares, nor the prophetick soule,
> Of the wide world, dreaming on things to come,
> Can yet the lease of my true loue controule,
> Supposde as forfeit to a confin'd doome.
> The mortall Moone hath her eclipse indur'de,
> And the sad Augurs mock their owne presage,
> Incertenties now crowne them-selues assur'de,
> And peace proclaimes Oliues of endlesse age.
> Now with the drops of this most balmie time,
> My loue lookes fresh, and death to me subscribes,
> Since spight of him Ile liue in this poore rime,
> While he insults ore dull and speachlesse tribes.
> And thou in this shalt finde thy monument,
> When tyrants crests and tombs of brasse are spent.

There is general agreement that the 'mortall Moone' stands for Queen Elizabeth, the Cynthia of Ralegh and after Ralegh Spenser, of whom Donne too wrote in his *Progresse of the Soule* of 1601, although this was not printed until 1633, as

> the great soule which here amongst us now
> Doth dwell, and moves that hand, and tongue, and brow,
> Which, as the Moone the sea, moves us.

Clearly, too, the sonnet was in part inspired by some contemporary peace or expectation of peace. The divergence of opinion is concerned with the nature of the 'eclipse', which the mortal moon 'hath indur'de'. An eclipse is a transitory thing. The *Oxford Dictionary* defines the noun in its derived senses as 'absence, cessation, or deprivation of light, temporary or permanent' and again as 'obscuration, obscurity; dimness; loss of brilliance or splendour', but none of its examples cover death. The verb it similarly defines as 'to cast a shadow upon, throw into the shade; to obscure, deprive of lustre', and adds, as an obsolete sense, 'to extinguish (life)'. And here it cites Shakespeare's *1 Henry VI* (IV. v. 52),

> Then here I take my leave of thee, fair son,
> Born to eclipse thy life this afternoon.

It is spoken by Lord Talbot to his son John, who in fact dies
in battle. This is Shakespeare's only use, outside our sonnet,
of 'eclipse' in the sense of death. There is no parallel in
Antony and Cleopatra (III. xiii. 153) where Antony says,

> Alack, our terrene moon
> Is now eclips'd; and it portends alone
> The fall of Antony!

If the moon is Cleopatra, she is not dead, and is in fact present,
but Antony thinks she has failed him. There may be an echo
of our sonnet in some lines ascribed to Sir John Davies, on the
death of James I in 1625,

> By that Eclipse which darkned our Appollo
> Our sunne did sett, and yett noe night did follow.

It is a very mixed metaphor.

If, then, 'eclipse' in the sonnet may possibly mean death,
what of 'hath indur'de'? From the *Oxford Dictionary*, again,
we get definitions of 'to endure' as 'to undergo, bear, sustain
(continuous pain, opposition, hardship or annoyance); *properly*,
to undergo without succumbing or giving way', and 'to suffer
without resistance, submit to, tolerate; to contemplate with
toleration'. No example of 'enduring death' is given. Shakespeare, however, who uses the word nearly a hundred times,
furnishes two. One is in *Lear* (v. ii. 9), 'Men must endure
Their going hence, even as their coming hither'. The other,
by implication at least, is in *Cymbeline* (v. v. 299),

> By thine own tongue thou art condemn'd, and must
> Endure our law. Thou'rt dead.

There are others, later, in Milton. Eve says of Adam (*Paradise
Lost*, IX. 832),

> So dear I love him, that with him all deaths
> I could endure, without him live no life.

Michael, again, says to Adam himself (*P.L.* XI. 364),

> so shalt thou lead
> Safest thy life, and best prepar'd endure
> Thy mortal passage when it comes.

It must be remembered that, in Christian thought, death is not
final, but only a transition to eternity. Shakespeare is less theo-
logical in his thought than Milton, but his 'going hence' is
much like Milton's 'passage', and it is possible, therefore, that
the 'hath indur'de' of the sonnet might refer to the death of

Elizabeth. On the other hand, it might equally well refer to some temporary overshadowing of her life, by illness or other danger, and in view of the linking of the eclipse in the same sentence with the happy expectation of peace and with the mocking of the augural presage, which a death would have confirmed, that seems to me to be on the whole the best interpretation. It may, however, be argued that what the augurs presaged was not the death itself, but the political difficulties to which it might give rise.

Theories as to the date of the sonnet have been somewhat biased by rival views as to the identity of the 'youth', on the one hand with Henry Wriothesley, Earl of Southampton, born on 6 October 1573, and William, Lord Herbert, later Earl of Pembroke, born on 8 April 1580. I need not discuss them here. In another paper I have attempted to put the case for Herbert. The sonnet itself has been variously ascribed to 1596, 1598, and 1603. The argument for 1596 was put most fully by Dr. G. B. Harrison in two articles on 'Shakespeare's Topical Significances', contributed to *The Times Literary Supplement* for 29 November 1928 and 13 November 1930, and in a section of 'The Passing of an Eclipse' in his *Shakespeare at Work* of 1933. He rather confused the issue by citing in support of it a letter by William Camden, preserved in Cotton Julius MS. c. iii, which contains a reference to an illness of Queen Elizabeth 'in this hir Clymactericall yeare'. The letter is only dated *15 Martii* in the MS., but other references in it show that it was clearly written during Elizabeth's last illness in 1603. And this is confirmed by an entry in Camden's *Annales* (ed. 1717), which records that the Queen died, 'annum agens climactericum, scilicet, septuagesimum'. Others, before Dr. Harrison, had fallen into the same error as to the date of the letter, but it is given correctly as of 1603 in Thomas Wright's *Queen Elizabeth and her Times* (1838), ii. 494. In reply to a criticism by me in *The Times Literary Supplement* for 25 January 1934, Dr. Harrison admitted his slip, but thought it immaterial to his main argument, which was that the 'eclipse' of the sonnet referred not to an illness of Elizabeth, but to an astrological threat of disaster to her during the year of her 'grand climacteric', upon which she entered on 7 September 1595. And in defence of this he cited a sermon by Anthony Rudde, Bishop of St. David's, delivered in the Queen's chapel on 9 April 1596, and described in Thomas Fuller's *Church History* (1655), and also in T. Park, *Nugae Antiquae* (1804), ii. 215, from a manuscript *Briefe View of the State of the Church of England*, written by Sir John Harington of Kelston in 1608. The bishop dwelt on sacred and mystical numbers, and in particular on those of 7 times 9 for the grand climacterical year, and was apparently indiscreet enough to suggest a prayer for the Queen, in which he included the words,

O Lord, I am now entered a good way into the climacterical year of mine age, which mine enemies wish and hope to be fatal unto me.

The Queen opened her closet window and, instead of giving him thanks for his sermon, said plainly,

He should have kept his arithmetick for himselfe; but I see the greatest clerks are not the wisest men.

Certainly the pseudo-philosophical writers of the sixteenth and seventeenth centuries were full of notions of climacterical or 'stayrie' years of life, which were regarded as dangerous. The word comes from the Greek κλιμακτήρ, the 'round of a ladder'. The theories took various forms, but stress was most often laid on every seventh year, sometimes also on every ninth or tenth. Thomas Wright, in 'a Succinct Philosophicall Declaration of the Nature of Clymactericall Yeeres, occasioned by the Death of Queene Elizabeth' (1604), appended to a revised edition of his *The Passions of the Minde in Generall* (1601), does not use the term 'grand climacteric', but he says,

The most daungerous of all these passages or steps, are the forty nine, compounded vpon seuen times seauen: and sixty three standing vppon nine times seauen, and next to these seauenty, which containeth tenne times seauen.

I should agree that the grand climacteric might be written of as an eclipse, but I think that Harrison is less convincing in his speculation that the 'incertenties' of the sonnet were caused by the strained relations between Elizabeth and Henri IV of France in January 1596, and the fall of Calais in April, and that they were 'assur'de' by the raid on Cadiz in June, and by a prospect of peace with its olives arising out of the new Triple Alliance between England, France, and the Netherlands in May. It is true that, when Henri entered Rouen to ratify the treaty on 6 October, he was met with a device in which an angel presented him with a sword of peace, and made a speech on the topic. Nevertheless, the whole object of the Triple Alliance was to continue the war with Spain.

Harrison's date was accepted by Mr. J. A. Fort in *A Time Scheme for Shakespeare's Sonnets* (1929), and 'The Order and Chronology of Shakespeare's Sonnets' (1933, *Review of English Studies*, ix. 19–23). There is even less to commend that of 1598 proposed by F. G. Fleay in his *Biographical Chronicle of the English Drama* (1891), ii. 221. He took the prospect of peace to have arisen from the treaty between France and Spain at Vervins on 2 May 1598. But this was entirely contrary to English interests. Elizabeth had done her best to avert it, and, although its terms left room for her adherence to it, she stood aloof, in spite of the advice of Lord Burghley. A more plausible date is that of 1603, the case for which has been put most recently by Dr. G. Mattingly (1933, *P.M.L.A.* xlviii. 705–21). This, of course, implies the acceptance of the eclipse as the death of the Queen. But certainly the augurs might well have presaged troubles to come at the change of dynasty. Spain was thought likely to intervene in support of the claims of her Infanta against those of James of Scotland. In England itself there were fears of risings by or against the Catholics. But all passed without disturbance. James loved to be called *Rex Pacificus*. By July 1603 he had opened negotiations for peace with Spain, although they did not lead to an actual treaty until July 1604. The symbolical olives recur in connexion with his coming. Sir John Harington welcomed Queen Anne on her arrival to join him in England, with an elegy, in which he wrote (McClure, *Letters and Epigrams of Sir John Harington*, 321),

> Like peacefull olive and like fruitfull vine,
> Yow banish dreadful war and barren dearth.

So, too, later, Gervase Markham, in his *Honour in His Perfection* (1624) tells of 'the incomparable King James', and adds,

> He enters not with an Olive branch in his hand, but with a whole Forrest of Olives round about him, for he brought not peace to this Kingdom alone, but almost to all the Christian Kingdomes of Europe.

Perhaps one might add Shakespeare's *Antony and Cleopatra* (iv. vi. 5), written about 1607, for confirmation of the significance of the imagery in the poet's mind,

> The time of universal peace is near.
> Prove this a prosperous day, the three-nook'd world
> Shall bear the olive freely.

The chief difficulty about taking 1603 as the date of *Sonnet* cvii is that it seems very late for any sonnet in the first series.

The 'youth' is still a 'sweet boy' in CVIII and a 'lovely boy' in
CXXVI, with which the series closes, and although Shakespeare
uses the term 'boy' very loosely in his plays, it does not seem
quite appropriate to a belted earl, such as Southampton, who
became 30 in 1603, or even to Pembroke, who then became 23.

I suggested 1599 as a plausible date in *The Year's Work in
English Studies* for 1928 (IX. 148), but it will be well to state
the case more in detail. The reign of Elizabeth is so full of
incident, that historians of her later years, intent upon Irish
complications and fascinated by the dramatic end of the pinch-
beck Earl of Essex, have been inclined to pass rather lightly
over other affairs which gave contemporary concern. There is,
however, abundant material available in archives, public and
private, notably in those of Sir Robert Cecil, Secretary of State
and in effect chief minister of the Crown, which are preserved
at Hatfield. The earlier part of the history of 1599 is mostly to
be gathered from the correspondence with Sir Henry Neville,
the English ambassador at Paris, and from 'advices', which
reached Cecil from travellers in Spain and similar sources and
remained confidential.

In 1598 a Spanish merchant *flota* had gone to the West
Indies for treasure, and would be due back towards the end of
1599. In January of that year some galleons were sent to escort
it. During the same month came news of a great concentration
of ships and soldiers at Lisbon and Cadiz, and of a belief there
that they were intended to take help to the rebellion of the
Earl of Tyrone in Ireland, and possibly to attack the Channel
Islands. England had no fleet at sea. The Dutch had, and in
February they promised that it should lie on the coasts of Spain,
and annoy hostile traffic. Early in March the Spanish concentration began to shift to Corunna and Ferrol at the north-west
angle of the country, and its size became considerable. Possibly its objective was now England itself, rather than Ireland.
In April Don Martin de Padilla, the Adelantado of Castile,
took charge. He wanted to obtain the use of the French harbour of Brest, but this Henry IV, anxious to be on good terms
with England as well as Spain, refused. Cecil was still relying
on the Dutch fleet, which on 22 May passed Plymouth towards
the west. This it would have to do, in order to reach the coast
of Galicia, but in fact it made no attempt at hostile or even
precautionary action against Spain itself, but sailed onwards to
the Spanish islands off the coast of Africa, where on 22 June

it took the Grand Canary and ravaged the settlers with extreme cruelty. This did not become known to Cecil until mid-July, and now he became extremely uneasy. The Dutch had failed him and England must take measures for her own protection against the Adelantado's array. On 1 August he moved swiftly. Two letters, a little later, to Sir Henry Neville, and to his friend John Manners in Derbyshire, explain his earlier attitude and his reasons for changing it. To Neville he wrote,

The reports from France, by the Governors of Deipe and of Calais, and from Monsieur de Sourdiac have bin such, as gave no small cause for us to apprehend some invasion from Spaine; considering that at that tyme both her Majestie's fleet was in harbour, and most of her commaunders in Ireland; but thanks be to God her Majesty's navy is now ready to set to sea, and she hath both an army in the west, and another here, ready eyther for Kent or Essex, with which we do but attend their coming; not doubting but to pay them their accustomed wages, which is ruine and contempt. These things I do tell you gave us this alarm, being these reports (whereof I send you herein the abstract) that you may see with what a whirlwind they were brought hither; though for my part yt was ever to me a paradox, that the fleet was in Brest; and yet all circumstances considered of my place and fortune, I did choose rather to run with the streame of providence, then of too much confidence upon myne own intelligences, which I must confess did assure me of preparations all the year, for defence against the State's fleet; of which I did ever think the enemy would make some use, so soon as he should be secure of them upon his owne coasts; a matter wherein they dealt unworthely with the Queene; for yf they had not promised to stay on that coast, her Majestie would have armed, as the King of Spaine did; but they for gaine transported themselves to the Canaries, which is a matter of no consequence, for now he hath gathered indeed a head at the Groyne [Corunna], whether according to his reports he should bring his gallies, you must judge that his desseign must be for England; but for my part I am not advertized that the gallies are so neer as the Groyne. Though when I consider that those I use are but the sons of Adam, and that yt is not impossible, but that they might be corrupted or deceaved, I have given way to these preparations that are made, preferring therein the wayes of safety, before any matter of charge. (E. Sawyer, *Memorials of Affairs of State*, i. 90.)

To Manners he wrote, similarly,

I have been constrayned to give more waye then I wold, because the world is ever apte to crye *crucifige* uppon me, as they have donne uppon my father before me, whensoever I doe diswade theise preperations, which bring soe great vexations to the people. This doe I wryte to you as a friend whoe have been longe acquaynted with the fortune of our

howse, and I must trewly add this further that, though the brutes that
have been brought from sea are more violent then are possible to be trewe,
yett we knowe this for certayne that they have prepared in Spayne
myghtely to resist the fleete of the Lowe Contreyes, which having now
left the coast and being gone for the Canaries, the Spaniards, that care not
for that place in respect of other desecggs [? designs] to better purpose,
wilbe apt enough to convert the forces prepared for the defensive, to
offend us whome they presume to fynde without any shippes at sea and
without any store of commaunders, things that will quicken the appetite
of malitious enemyes. (*H.M.C. Report on Belvoir Castle MSS.*, i. 356.)

By 1 August preparations against an invasion were in full
swing. Ships were available at Chatham and Gravesend, and a
fleet could be ready to go to sea in a fortnight. Lord Howard
de Walden was appointed Admiral, with Sir Walter Ralegh
as Vice-Admiral and Fulke Greville as Rear-Admiral. A commission was issued for the impressment of mariners. Some
were sent from Plymouth. Sir Robert Sidney must bring others
from Flushing. Behind the fleet an army would be concentrated in a camp at Tilbury. Lord Cobham, the Warden of the
Cinque Ports, would fortify Margate and the Downs. The
Earl of Bath was in command in Devonshire and Sir William
Russell in Hampshire. Special letters were issued by the Privy
Council to noblemen and a few gentlemen, such as Sir Henry
Lee, to furnish a bodyguard of horse, for the protection of the
Queen's person. It must be ready by 20 August. The City of
London must provide for its own safety, and that of the Thames
estuary. Sir Thomas Gerard would command. But the City
had an old grudge against him, and the Earl of Cumberland
was substituted. He had a device for making a fortified bridge
over the river at Gravesend, which proved impracticable. So
did another of sinking hulks in the channel. It would block
traffic for years and drown the marshes. Finally it was decided
to be content with placing ordnance on the banks at Blackwall
and elsewhere, and leaving some small fighting craft on the
river itself. A watch was kept upon Catholic recusants, who
might cause mischief. The Archbishop of Canterbury proposed a special form of prayers. That used at the time of the
Spanish Armada would, he thought, be suitable. And in about
three weeks all was over. On 15 August the Adelantado sailed.
He made no attempt at invasion, but went south to meet the
Dutch. Storms drove him back, and by December he was in
Lisbon with a weather-beaten fleet. He had left only a few light

galleys behind him in August. It was feared that they might attempt to come up the Thames, but this came to nothing. By 23 August the English fleet was at sea. The land forces, except in the west, were being discharged. The assembly of the Queen's bodyguard, several times put off, was finally abandoned. Cecil and England breathed freely.

There is little evidence of widespread uneasiness in England during the first half of 1599. Cecil naturally kept his advices to himself and Neville, and if anything from his informants leaked out, it does not seem to have got very far. Possibly the burning of Penzance, Newlyn, and Mousehole during a Spanish raid of 1595 had not been forgotten in the west. Certainly the officers in charge of Plymouth, Falmouth, and the Scilly Isles and those in Jersey and Guernsey were on the alert. But it was not until the sudden preparations of August that any general scare arose. John Chamberlain, writing from London to Dudley Carleton at Ostend about the academic Commencement at Cambridge, tells him,

Perhaps verses and schollerlike exercises may be welcome in the middes of warres, the alarme wherof begins to ringe in our eares here at home as shrill as in your beseiged towne. For, upon what grounde or goode intelligence I know not, but we are all here in a hurle as though the ennemie were at our doores. (*Letters*, 56.)

A little later he refers to the 'scambling provisions and preparations for warre', and adds,

Upon Monday, toward evening, came newes (yet false) that the Spaniardes were landed in the Ile of Wight, which bred such a feare and consternation in this towne as I wold litle have looked for, with such a crie of women, chaining of streets, and shutting of the gates, as though the ennemie had ben at Blackewall. I am sory and ashamed that this weakenes and nakednes of ours on all sides shold shew itself so apparently as to be carried far and neere, to our disgrace both with frends and foes. (*Letters*, 58–9.)

Naturally, in such a state of things, wild rumours spread over the country. The Privy Council sent many letters to the Lord Mayor, ordering their suppression and the apprehension of their authors. A London citizen, writing to Cecil, furnishes examples of them.

As that the Spaniard's fleet is 150 sail of ships and 70 gallies; that they bring 30,000 soldiers with them, and shall have 20,000 from the Cardinal; that the King of Denmark sends to aid him 100 sail of ships; that the King of Scots is in arms with 40,000 men to invade England, and the Spaniard comes to settle the King of Scots in this realm: which is so creditably bruited as a preacher, in his prayer before his sermon, prayed to be delivered from the mighty forces of the Spaniard, the Scots, and the Danes; that my Lord Scroope was slain, with 200 men more, by the Scots; that Sir William Bowes was turned out of Scotland by the King with great disdain; that the Adilantado has taken the sacrament to come to London Bridge, and brings his wife and two daughters with him. Upon Tuesday at night last, it went for certain the Spaniards were landed at Southampton, and that the Queen came at ten of the clock at night to St. James's in all post; and upon Wednesday, it was said the Spanish army was broken, and no purpose of their coming hither: with 100 other strange and fearful rumours, as much amazing the people as the invasion were made. (*Cal. Hatfield MSS.* ix. 282.)

But here is no mention of the most alarming and widespread rumour of all, which was that the Queen herself was either dead, or at least dangerously ill. She was now 65 and was beginning to feel her age and to resent any mention of it. As a matter of fact, she seems to have been quite well throughout 1599, but for a slight indisposition on 14 January, which caused her to put off an audience. On Twelfth Night she had been dancing with the Earl of Essex at court, to do honour to the Danish ambassador. She bade him tell his king 'that she was not so infirm that she could not still dance and do other things that pertain to a vigorous active body' and in a later audience added, 'Those who think I am an invalid egg him on as far as they can'. In July a progress was extended 'by reason of an intercepted letter, wherein the giving over of long voyages was noted to be sign of age'. The letter happens to exist. It was written to Venice by a resident in London, who said that she rode with difficulty, but was 'in health, though more than usually subject to fretting and melancholy'. In September the Scottish ambassador wrote to his king,

At her majesty's returning from Hampton Court, the day being passing foul, she would (as her custom is) go on horseback, although she is scarce able to sit upright, and my lord Hunsdon said, 'It was not meet for one of her Majesty's years to ride in such a storm'. She answered, in great anger, 'My years! Maids, to your horses quickly'; and so rode all the way, not vouchsafing any gracious countenance to him for two days. (F. Chamberlin, *Private Character of Queen Elizabeth*, 72.)

She was an indomitable old lady. Abroad, however, there were reports that she was dangerously ill. At Venice, in January, it was believed that she had a cancer, and could not live long. Perhaps some such story came to the ears of Henri IV, who was favourably disposed to her, and made many inquiries as to her health, both through Neville and through his own ambassador in England, M. de Boissise. In July and August the Spaniards at Lisbon and Corunna were comforting themselves with the assurance that she was even dead. Venice had heard the same. And it was clearly this rumour, perhaps deliberately circulated by the Catholic recusants, which caused most consternation in England itself. On 15 August one Richard Gibbons wrote from St. Omer in France to Fano in Italy.

In England there is tumult and fear, and many fly into the southern parts. Some say that the Queen is dead, it is certain that there is great mourning at court, and messengers are sent to France in haste. (*Cal. State Papers, Domestic*, 272/47.)

On 11 August Rowland Whyte wrote to Sir Robert Sidney that the Queen was 'very well and nothing dismaied at all these rumours'. By 15 August they had got as far as Cornwall. Here Richard Pearne of Peran Arwothal had been told by William Crowsyer of Gwennap that she was dead and that an army was in the field about London, where her picture was brought out, but she was not there in person. The warden of Pendennis Castle sent him to jail, and notified Cecil that the country was much troubled with rumour-spreaders and other idle persons. But it is from Buckinghamshire that most of the records come. On 13 August Jasper Oseley met at Hanslope one Humfrey Stafford of Westbury, who said he had heard credibly that there were no Spaniards, but that the mustering was for a worse matter.

'What is that?' said I, and Stafford answered, 'The Queen is either dead or dangerously sick', and in the end he did affirm to me that the Queen was dead. At which words I greatly grieved. (*Cal. Hatfield MSS*. ix. 428.)

On 16 August Henry Wake of Sawcy in Northants, wrote to Cecil of a similar report, secretly spread and whispered, and added that the beginners of such speeches were dwellers in Bucks, outside the limits of his jurisdiction. But he could give their names, if desired. The Queen was angry with Wake for not arresting his informant, and said that, if he could not produce the author of the report, he was worthy of severe punishment. 'And, to tell you truly', wrote Sir John Stanhope, the Treasurer of her Chamber, she 'was never quiet since'. Later it seems to have been alleged that this author was William

Fortescue, the son of no less a person than Sir John Fortescue of Salden, the Chancellor of the Exchequer, who wrote in some perturbation and rather obscurely. William was now gone to the sea.

I presume he would not make any such slanderous report, having seen her Majesty walk in the garden and hunt in the park the day before his departure. But, under correction, Mr. Wake, who seems to me to be author, for that he layeth it in generality that some that came from me should give out such speech, would be sent for to make particular expression of the party's name whom he accuses, and so the matter might be tried out and severely punished in the author and spreader of the rumour. I have sent for my son to answer anything that may be to him objected, who if he cannot clear himself, I will utterly reject him. (*Cal. Hatfield MSS.* ix. 314.)

Sir Henry Lee, of Quarrendon, travelling to court, sent to Cecil his servant Bennet Wilson, who had also heard a version of the rumour from Thomas Allyne at Winslow. He was ready to examine the parties, if Cecil so desired. To Dudley Carleton John Chamberlain wrote on 23 August,

The vulgar sort cannot be perswaded but that there was some great misterie in the assembling of these forces, and because they cannot finde the reason of it make many wilde conjectures, and cast beyond the moone; as sometimes that the Quene was daungerously sicke, otherwhile that it was to shew to some that are absent [Essex, of course] that others can be followed as well as they, and that if occasion be, militarie services can be as well and redily ordered and directed as if they were present, with many other as vaine and frivolous imaginations as these. (*Letters*, 62.)

But the last word was with Elizabeth herself. On 29 August Whyte wrote to Sidney,

Her Majesty is in very good health, and likes well of Nonsuch ayre. Long may she continue souveraine lady over this poore land. Here hath many rumors been bruted of her, which troubled her Majestie a litle, for she wold say, *Mortua sed non sepulta*. (*H.M.C. Report on Penshurst MSS.* ii. 385.)

I cannot help comparing the casting beyond the moon of Chamberlain's letter with the lines of Shakespeare's sonnet,

> The mortall Moone has her eclipse indur'de,
> And the sad Augurs mock their owne presage.

Nor were the olives of peace lacking. It is curious that throughout this year of naval alarms negotiations for peace were constantly in progress. Philip II of Spain had died on 13 September 1598. His son Philip III was a young and idle

man, devoted to his pleasures. It was believed that he would
be pacific. The sovereignty of the Netherlands had been left
to his sister Isabella, the Infanta, who was betrothed to the
Archduke Albert of Austria. They would not be wealthy, and
the charges of war with England and the Dutch were heavy.
The marriage took place on 13 November, but the bridal pair
came slowly through Italy, and did not arrive at their capital
until the September of 1599. As early, however, as November
1598 negotiations for peace had been opened with Elizabeth
by Cardinal Andreas, their Deputy in the Netherlands, who
sent one Jerome Coomans, a counsellor of Antwerp, to London.
No immediate result followed, but in the summer of 1599
Coomans was again passing between England and Spain, and
by the middle of August Philip had given the Archduke liberty
to treat. The prospect of an agreement now became a matter
of common knowledge in England. 'Here is a mutring of a
peace', wrote Whyte to Sir Robert Sidney, 'God grant it may
be profitable to our poor country.' So too Chamberlain noted,
'In the middest of all this hurle burle here is a sodain sound of
peace'. But there were considerable difficulties to be sur-
mounted. The goodwill of Henri IV was desirable. He offered
Elizabeth advice, adding that 'he knew her to be so wise, and
so well assisted by wise Counsail, as she little needed his'. But
Neville at least suspected his *bona fides*, believing that he
desired to step into her place as protector of the Dutch. More
important was the attitude of the Dutch themselves, complicated by the Queen's unwillingness to surrender the cautionary
towns which she held in their country, without some other
security for the repayment of her loans. After long negotiations they refused to stand in, and in December Elizabeth
decided to proceed alone. She would have liked a peace conference to be held in England, but to this the Archduke would
not agree, and it was decided that it should take place on neutral
ground at Boulogne during May 1600. Long before it met
there was much scepticism as to whether it would lead to anything. 'Whatsoever the reason is, methincks we are not so hot
on this peace as we were', wrote Chamberlain on 29 February.
On 1 April Cecil thought the Archduke's suggestions prepos-
terous. He wanted the Queen to give up the cautionary towns,
not to the Dutch, but to him, and to abandon all commercial
intercourse with the States. It was feared in Scotland that he
would ask to have the Infanta, rather than King James, ac-

cepted 'pro sole oriente', as Elizabeth's successor. Clearly there was no real foundation on which to build a peace. The delegates met, however, as arranged, and on 28 July broke up, nominally on a disagreement as to the historical claims of the English and Spanish representatives for formal precedence.

The most likely date for the 'Mortal Moon' sonnet is, I think, August 1599, when the prospect of olives began to dawn. It might, however, have been written at any time between that and the end of February 1600, but hardly later, when the hope for peace must have been rapidly waning.

1943.

NOTE

The main records, on which this essay is based, may be found in the Historical Manuscripts Commission volumes on the *Hatfield MSS.* (ix, *passim*; x. 6, 10, 36, 93, 125, 145, 166, 167); on the *Penshurst MSS.* (ii, *passim*); on the *Belvoir MSS.* (i. 355, 356); on the *Savile-Foljambe MSS.* (66–98); in the *Calendar of Domestic State Papers* (270/96, 97, 119; 271/33, 35, 106, 113, 114, 140; 272/5, 7, 18, 47, 49, 94; 273/1); in the *Calendar of Venetian Papers*, ix. 355, 369; in E. Sawyer, *Memorials of Affairs of State*, i. 16–175, *passim*; 186–226; in John Chamberlain's *Letters*, 38, 56, 58, 61, 66, 67, 73, 75, 81; in P. P. Laffleur de Kermaingant, *L'Ambassade de Jean de Thumery*, i. 250, 253, 257, 258; ii. 45, 62; in E. Lodge, *Illustrations of British History* (ed. 2), ii. 524, 532; in A. Collins, *Letters and Memorials of State*, ii. 114, 115, 382; in V. von Klarwill, *2 Fugger Letters*, 313, 315, 319; in N. E. McClure, *Letters and Epigrams of Sir John Harington*, 80; in F. Chamberlin, *The Private Character of Queen Elizabeth*, 72; in *The Times* (29. x. 1924). *Vide* also my *Sir Henry Lee* (1936), 173–4.

SHAKESPEARE AT CORPUS

(The following has been sent us by an esteemed contributor, and therefore we print it. But, as St. Augustine said about the legend of the Pelican, 'This may be true, it may be false'. EDD. *P.R.*)

SHAKESPEARE's knowledge of classics and philosophy has always puzzled his biographers. A few years at the Stratford Grammar School do not explain it, yet no one has drawn the obvious conclusion, that Shakespeare was a University man. Tradition records that he visited Oxford and was on friendly terms with the Davenants, who then kept what was afterwards the Crown Inn in the Corn-Market. What more likely than that he was up as an Undergraduate, and was led to that hostelry in search of liquid refreshment after a lecture by Ludovicus Vivès on the *Posterior Analytics*? It is easy, as this paper will prove, to show that his plays are filled with reminiscences of University life. But, if he was at Oxford at all, he must of course have been at Corpus. Where else could he have gone? Was not Corpus the characteristic outcome of the Renaissance? Did not the great Erasmus himself say that as Rhodes was famous for its Colossus, and Caria for its Mausoleum, even so should Corpus be among the chief ornaments of Britain? There is a plain allusion to this prophecy in the words of Cassius (who is Shakespeare), about Caesar (who perhaps signifies the College), 'Why, man, he doth bestride the narrow world, Like a Colossus'.[1] Moreover, Corpus was a haunt of poets. Richard Edwards was here, and Nicholas Udall. Spenser was here, not indeed the author of the *Faerie Queene*, but his cousin, or at least a man of the same name as his cousin.[2] Surely the youthful Shakespeare, conscious already of his poetic genius, would have been here too! Internal evidence shows that he *was* here. Touchstone, in *As You Like It*, offers to 'Stand to it, the pancakes were naught and the mustard was good'.[3] Now every one knows that the Corpus mustard is good, as indeed it should be, seeing that we pay 4*s*. a term for 'cruets', and no one who has been in Hall on Shrove-Tuesday will deny that 'the pancakes were

---

[1] *Julius Caesar*, I. ii. 135. My friend, Prof. Piffelwitz, of Berlin, would read 'Like a Corpus', but, though the *ductus literarum* favours the emendation, the line would be difficult to scan.

[2] Vide *The Spending of the Money of Roger Nowell*.   [3] *A.Y.L.* I. ii. 69.

naught'. Clearly, then, Touchstone (that is of course Shakespeare) was a Corpus man. Then, again, there is frequent mention in the plays of Foxes and of Bees, of the Presidential Tortoise, that original of Caliban,[1] and of the late lamented Senior Fellow. He is the 'Poor Tom' of the Mad scenes in *King Lear*,[2] who was 'a-cold', and haunted by nightingales, who fed upon 'rats and mice and such small deer' and was the natural foe of the little dogs, 'Tray, Blanch, and Sweetheart'. It can only be by a curious lapse of memory that Edgar (probably Shakespeare) says, 'Pur! the cat is *gray*'. We have also the familiar Corpus birds, the Owl and the Pelican, and it is noteworthy that Shakespeare uses the name 'Pelicock', a variant for 'Pelican', which is, I believe, local and unique. In a scene of *King Lear*, just quoted, the quartos read correctly, 'Pelicock sat on Pelicock-hill',[3] the hill being of course the mound on which the sun-dial in the quad once stood. The folio editors, not being Corpus men, missed the point and spoilt the sense by a reading of their own. Such alterations are common in the folio text. It is well known that all profanities were cut out, in obedience to an Act of James I, but it has not, I think, been observed before that, owing to that monarch's notorious dislike for tobacco, a number of allusions to the 'nicotian herb' have also been suppressed. Thus, in *Julius Caesar*,[4] we find 'the honey-heavy dew of slumber'. Originally the line must have run 'the heavy honey-dew of slumber'. The folio reading is simple nonsense. The specific gravity of honey is considerably above that of H_2O or water, a fact which Shakespeare must have known, if his editors did not.

Life at Corpus in the sixteenth century seems to have been very like that of our own day. Familiar words are sprinkled over the poet's lines; 'commons' and 'commoners', 'messengers' and 'scouts' and 'battels'. 'Battels', by the way, the folio editors always mis-spell 'battles', though the phrase 'A battel, when they charge on heaps'[5] might have saved them from that error. From *Macbeth* we learn that, then too, men knocked the porter up at midnight, and that the Owlet Club held its weekly meetings, or, as Shakespeare puts it, 'the

---

[1] *Tempest*, I. ii. 316, where Caliban is addressed by Prospero-Shakespeare, 'Come, thou tortoise! when?' Mr. Ignatius Donnelly believes that Caliban was Shakespeare himself. Perhaps he was his scout.

[2] *Lear*, III. iv. 59, 144, 177; III. vi. 31, 47, 66. [3] *Lear*, III. iv. 78.

[4] *Julius Caesar*, II. i. 230. [5] *Tr. Cr.*, III. ii. 29.

obscure bird Clamoured the livelong night'.[1] This last fact may startle some readers who think that they remember the birth of the Owlet Club; but they should reflect that Shakespeare knew many things that they didn't know that he knew. Personally I had always regarded the Primrose League as a modern institution, until I found him speaking of 'the primrose way to the everlasting bonfire'.[2]

Shakespeare was never a bookworm. He alludes to the Stratford School with some distaste as a place where 'none will sweat but for promotion',[3] and in Oxford he read but little. When he speaks of himself as one that 'hath been tutored in the Rudiments',[4] we gather that he had to put on a coach for an examination that in our day has not been held to require it. In his last year he received from a friend the warning, 'Thou art so near the gulph',[5] and there is reason to believe that, in the end, he was actually ploughed. That, at least, is the natural inference from the words of Titinius (perhaps an examiner) to Cassius (Shakespeare), 'Alas, thou hast misconstrued everything'.[6] Shakespeare is Cassius and Prospero and Edgar and Touchstone, but still more is he Polonius. Polonius is a University man, and has enacted Julius Caesar for the Oxford University Dramatic Society.[7] He can give good counsel to Laertes, as one who has been there. Above all, he advises him not to give fresher-breakfasts; 'do not dull thy palm with entertainment Of each new-fledged unhatched comrade'. Hamlet addresses him somewhat rudely as 'Buz, Buz'.[9] Probably this was the usual nickname of Corpus men, owing to the fact that at Oldham's suggestion they took the place of a company of 'buzzing' or 'bussing' monks.[10] Almost in his last moments, mindful of the days when he sat as senior scholar in the Corpus Hall, Polonius makes the apparently irrelevant remark, 'I'll sconce me'.[11] Surely he can be none other than Shakespeare himself.

Shakespeare tells us less than could be wished about his college contemporaries. It is surprising to learn that Oldham once held the office of President of Corpus, but in *Richard III*, the Messenger, who must have known, speaks distinctly of 'the haughty Pre, late Bishop of Exeter'.[12] Here the folio

---

[1] *Macb.*, ii. iii. 1, 64.   [2] Ibid., ii. iii. 21.   [3] *A.Y.L.* ii. iii. 60.
[4] Ibid., v. iv. 31.   [5] *Henry V*, iv. iii. 82.   [6] *Julius Caesar*, v. iii. 84.
[7] *Hamlet*, iii. ii. 108.   [8] Ibid., i. iii. 64.   [9] Ibid., ii. ii. 412.
[10] Holinshed, *Chronicles*. [11] *Hamlet*, iii. iv. 4. [12] *Richard III*, iv. iv. 502.

editors have as usual perverted the meaning, this time by omitting a comma. Fellows of the college are often mentioned, but never by name. I doubt if Shakespeare had a high opinion of them, as a body. 'Nature', he says, 'hath framed strange Fellows in her time'.[1] There were among them 'learned and authentic Fellows'[2] and 'a Fellow of infinite jest';[3] but there were also 'a periwig-pated Fellow',[4] 'a very scurvy Fellow',[5] 'a snipt-taffeta Fellow',[6] and an 'old fat Fellow'.[7] Probably this is 'the Fellow with the great belly', of *2 Henry IV*,[8] the prototype of Falstaff, and possibly also the 'Fellow in the cellarage' of *Hamlet*.[9] No doubt he was quite a character in his day.

1891.

[1] *Merchant of Venice*, i. i. 51.
[2] *All's Well*, ii. iii. 14.
[3] *Hamlet*, v. i. 203.
[4] Ibid., iii. ii. 10.
[5] *M. for M.*, v. i. 136.
[6] *All's Well*, iv. v. 1.
[7] *Merry Wives*, iv. iv. 15.
[8] *2 Henry IV*, i. ii. 165.
[9] *Hamlet*, i. v. 151.